ARMOURED RECONNAISSANCE

Traditionally, the role of the cavalry has been two-fold: first, to provide a shock force capable of breaking enemy lines and exploiting that breakthrough and, second, to act as a commander's eyes and ears by scouting ahead and identifying enemy positions and movements. Since the early twentieth century, there are two schools of thought in regard to this latter role: reconnaissance by force – heavily armoured forces able to identify and engage enemy forces – and reconnaissance by stealth – a lightly armoured, fast-moving force, able to defend itself but ill equipped to engage the enemy offensively. Historically, the British Army has favoured reconnaissance by stealth over reconnaissance by force and in the years between the two World Wars it favoured the wheeled armoured vehicle, the armoured car, to fulfil its reconnaissance needs.

At the beginning of World War II, the reconnaissance units of British armoured brigades were equipped with the Universal Carrier, as well as Vickers Light Tanks. Following the defeat in France in the summer of 1940, the armoured divisions forming in the United Kingdom included an armoured car regiment which would act as the divisional reconnaissance unit, while armoured reconnaissance in the Western Division continued to be provided by light tanks at brigade level. In 1942 an armoured car regiment was added to the establishment of armoured divisions serving in North Africa. The importance of armoured reconnaissance was recognised in 1941 with the formation of the Reconnaissance Corps, which provided an armoured car battalion for each infantry division. In 1944 the Reconnaissance Corps was transferred to the Royal Armoured Corps. In the armoured divisions the armoured car regiment was replaced by an armoured reconnaissance regiment in 1943. These reconnaissance regiments used a wide array of wheeled and tracked vehicles. The Reconnaissance Corps scout troops relied heavily on the Universal Carrier and Humber Light Reconnaissance Car at first, and later their strength was augmented by adoption of the Daimler Dingo, AEC and Staghound armoured cars. In the armoured divisions, reconnaissance was largely provided by tracked armoured vehicles, including the M3 and M5 light tanks and the A27M Cromwell.

At the end of the war, the reconnaissance units of the infantry divisions were disbanded and those of the armoured regiments much reduced. Although the Cromwell remained in service until the mid 1950s, the British Army favoured wheeled armoured reconnaissance vehicles in the post-war period. A host of obsolete armoured car types soldiered on well into the 1950s, notably the AEC Armoured Car Mk II. In 1952 the diminutive four-wheeled FV701 Ferret Armoured Car entered service and saw service with armoured reconnaissance regiments of the Royal Armoured Corps in the UK, with the British Army of the Rhine (BAOR) in Germany, and overseas in Malaya and Aden. In 1958 the

(below) The FV601 Saladin armoured car began to replace the AEC Armoured Car in the reconnaissance troops of the Royal Armoured Corps from 1958 onwards. (M P Robinson)

Saladin armoured cars of A Squadron, The Queen's Dragoon Guards, take position near Sheikh Othman in Yemen during the Aden Emergency in 1967. (Brian Harrington Spier)

six-wheeled FV601 Alvis Saladin entered service with the British Army. Armed with a 76mm L5A1 gun, it served with the BAOR and saw action during the Aden Emergency between 1963 and 1967 and with 16th/5th The Queen's Royal Lancers during the Turkish invasion of Cyprus in 1974. At some eleven tons in weight, the Saracen was a heavy vehicle and while its 76mm High-Explosive Squash Head (HESH) round was reasonably effective against conventionally armoured forces, its cross-country mobility was limited, especially in Germany. It was was too cumbersome to be airlifted to the various overseas commitments Britain still had east of the Suez Canal as the UK looked to reduce the number of expensive permanent overseas garrisons. By the mid 1960s these imperatives led to the search for a new armoured reconnaissance vehicle that could meet the strategic and operational needs of the British Army.

(below) The diminutive Ferret armoured car which also equipped the armoured reconnaissance regiments in the 1960s and early 1970s. This vehicle of C Squadron, 17th/21st Lancers was photographed at Crossmaglen in Northern Ireland in July 1973. In the same month, the rest of the regiment, stationed in Germany, received its third delivery of Scorpion. (Kevin Shannon)

THE DEVELOPMENT OF THE CVR(T)

By the late 1950s there was a growing recognition of the need for a next-generation armoured reconnaissance vehicle to replace Saladin and Ferret. This new vehicle would need to be air-portable and amphibious, with good cross-country capabilities and sufficient firepower and armour to operate on future European battlefields. Several feasibility studies were conducted at the Fighting Vehicles Research and Development Establishment (FVRDE) at Chertsey in Surrey, and these resulted, in 1960, in the Armoured Vehicle Reconnaissance programme. This envisaged a multi-role wheeled or tracked platform with a three-man crew and armed with either a 76mm or 105mm gun and Swingfire anti-tank guided missiles (ATGM). This ambitious project was too heavy to be air-portable and did not progress beyond the drawing board, but some of the ideas would resurface in the later CVR(T) programme. Given the United Kingdom's continuing post-colonial commitments, the need for air-portability remained of paramount concern. Simultaneously FVRDE was developing a lightweight self-propelled carriage for the 105mm howitzer. This was rejected by the Royal Artillery, but its chassis provided the basis for the Lightweight High Mobility Tracked Vehicle family (LHMTVF). This family of 4.5-ton vehicles included an APC, a 120mm recoilless rifle carrier, an armoured ambulance and a reconnaissance detachment carrier. The most important technological development during these early years was the adoption of the idea of aluminium-based armour, first introduced in the American M113 APC in 1959. This allowed the same ballistic protection and stability as steel armour at a fraction of the weight and allowed the need for air-portability to remain a viable option for the new armoured vehicles. In the early 1960s the FVRDE also successfully fitted the 4.2-litre Jaguar XK engine into a Ferret armoured car in place of its original Rolls Royce engine. Subsequent testing demonstrated that the powerful Jaguar engine could be used in AFVs more generally.

In 1965 a prototype vehicle, the TV15000 was built at Chertsey. Completed by Christmas, it had an aluminium hull, and the following year had its Rolls Royce engine replaced by a Jaguar one in the wake of the successful tests on Ferret. This prototype was instrumental in confirming the feasibility of a lightweight, air-portable armoured reconnaissance vehicle with sufficient survivability and which could fulfil the required range of battlefield roles. Five road wheels and new lightweight aluminium tracks gave it superb cross-country abilities and speeds of up to 50mph (80kmh) on roads. It was decided to develop two vehicle types: one with a 76mm gun fitted in a fully rotating turret and one armed with Swingfire ATGM. The need for adequate protection against heavy machine guns meant the weight limit had to rise to 17,500lbs (7.81 tons). This allowed for air-portability in the new C-130 Lockheed Hercules aircraft which the RAF had recently procured. This requirement for air-portability was the principal determinant of the vehicle's maximum weight and dimensions. Two further test rigs were built to test the automotive and cooling functions of the new design, now known as Combat Vehicle Reconnaissance (Tracked) (CVR(T)), and in September 1967 Alvis Limited of Coventry were awarded a contract to develop seventeen prototypes

One of the Scorpion prototypes undergoing testing at Military Vehicles and Engineering Establishment (MVEE), Chertsey. (MoD via Richard Stickland)

The Scimitar prototype at MVEE. The most rigorous testing of the CVR(T) hull and automotive components was carried out abroad, especially in Australia and Canada, on the Scorpion prototypes. (MoD via Richard Stickland)

of the new armoured reconnaissance vehicle, designated FV101 Scorpion. Alvis had a successful track record of defence production, having previously made the Saladin armoured car and Saracen APC, as well as the Stalwart High Mobility Load Carrier. A further six prototypes were to be built of the other proposed vehicles in the CVR(T) family. These included a close reconnaissance version armed with a 30mm Rarden cannon, an anti-tank vehicle armed with Swingfire ATGM, an APC, an armoured ambulance, a command post vehicle and a recovery vehicle.

The first Scorpion prototype left the Alvis factory on 23 January 1969. By May 1970 all the prototypes had been built. The prototypes underwent extensive testing in a variety of environments ranging from the deserts of Dubai and Australia, where temperatures reached 52°C, to the sub-artic conditions of Norway and Canada, where temperatures fell to -32°C. The testing was rigorous indeed with no fewer than 95,578 miles between February 1969 and April 1972. This included 26,670 miles on a high-speed test track and 25,095 over poor terrain. Extensive testing of the weapons systems was also conducted, with over 3,560 test firings. In May 1970 the CVR(T) was formally accepted for service with the British Army and on 30 July that year Alvis was awarded an initial contract for 275 Scorpion and 288 Scimitar. At the same time the British Army accepted the FV721 Fox Combat Vehicle Reconnaissance (Tracked) for service. This was a four-wheeled armoured car chassis built by Daimler, fitted with a similar (but not identical) 30mm Rarden cannon-armed turret as fitted to Scimitar. Alvis assembled these turrets too.

This early stage of development was also carried out with international partners and potential customers of the CVR(T) family in mind. While the prototypes were still undergoing testing, the Belgian government signed a Memorandum of Understanding whereby they undertook to purchase a proportion of the CVR(T)s to be manufactured by Alvis. Belgium firms in return supplied components for the CVR(T)s to be assembled in Coventry, and in October 1970 the Belgian government placed an order for some 700 CVR(T) vehicles. Similarly, one of the reasons that two Scorpions were flown to Queensland in November 1969 was the hope that the Australian government would agree to purchase the CVR(T) family. Unfortunately, during these trials, a Scorpion overturned when a track broke and an Australian serviceman was killed. Scorpion was also later demonstrated to the Lebanese and two vehicles were also sent to Iran, where they impressed, and orders duly placed by the Shah's government.

(above) A pristine-looking early FV102 Striker. The Swingfire missile system is raised in the firing position. Note the extended mudguards and the flotation screen still in place. (Richard Stickland)

THE CVR(T) FAMILY

From the early days of the Armoured Vehicle Reconnaissance (AVR) and Lightweight High Mobility Tracked Vehicle programmes, the idea of a single platform that could accommodate a variety of different hull designs performing various battlefield roles had been at the forefront of the designers' minds. From the beginning of the AVR programme a total of seven different vehicles were envisaged. These were: the AVR Fire support, which would become Scorpion; the AVR Anti-APC, which would develop into Scimitar; an AVR anti-tank capable of engaging enemy heavy armour; a liaison vehicle to replace Ferret; an APC to carry recce troops; a command vehicle; and an armoured ambulance.

Once Scorpion and Scimitar had been accepted into service, prototypes of the other CVR(T) family vehicles were manufactured and put through extensive trials at the Military Vehicles and Engineering Establishment (MVEE) at Chertsey, Surrey. The separate liaison vehicle was dropped, but the others were delivered to the British Army from the mid 1970s onwards. The first to be fielded was the FV102 Striker CVR(T) Anti-Tank Guided Weapon Launcher which entered service in 1976. It was based on the extended chassis of Scorpion and the same hull as the Spartan APC and carried five Swingfire wire-guided ATGMs. The three-man crew – driver, commander and missile operator – could also fire the missiles dismounted from the vehicle. Swingfire could engage targets up to 4,000km and was effective against all Soviet armour then in service. Like most similar systems, the missiles could only be reloaded externally, meaning a crew member had to dismount to do so. Originally, the Striker was to serve with the armoured reconnaissance regiments, but in the reorganisation of the British Army's armoured divisions in 1976-77, the new Striker batteries came under the control of the Royal Horse Artillery. Striker returned to Royal Armoured Corps control in 1984. From 2000, Striker was subject to the Life Extension Programme (LEP) applied to all CVR(T) and received the Cummins 6BTA 5.9-litre, six-cylinder diesel engine in place of its original 4.2-litre Jaguar petrol engine. Striker saw action in both Gulf Wars and in March 2003 a Striker of the Household Cavalary Regiment was credited with destroying an Iraqi T-55. 89 Striker were built between 1974 and 1986 and it was retired from service in 2005, the role subsequently being fulfilled by dismounted teams armed with the Javelin ATGM.

The most numerous CVR(T) was the FV103 Spartan Armoured Personnel Carrier, introduced in 1978 as a replacement for the FV603 Saracen. 691 Spartan were built up to 1986. The Spartan was based on a Scorpion chassis lengthened by 260mm. It has a three-man crew: commander, driver and a third crewman who is either a radio operator or the commander of the four-man recce squad who are seated in the rear of the vehicle. Spartan was also used by the

(left) An FV103 Spartan of 1st The Queen's Dragon Guards waits on the dock in Split, Croatia before deployment to Bosnia with NATO's Implementation Force in January 1996. (US Army photo by Sgt. Brian Gavin)

An FV104 Samaritan of The King's Royal Hussars during Exercise Lion Strike on Salisbury Plain in 2013. (MoD Crown Copyright photograph by Cpl Si Longworth RLC)

RAF who procured 81 to provide security for forward airfields in Germany operating Harrier. From 1984 67 Spartan were converted into CVR(T) MILAN Compact Turret, designed to carry thirteen MILAN ATGMs, including two ready to launch in the turret. These vehicles were assigned to the support companies of armoured infantry battalions before the introduction of FV510 Warrior IFVin 1988. 35 of these CVR(T) MCT were subsequently used in the OPFOR role at British Army Training Unit Suffield (BATUS) and designated CVR(T) Sturgeon. Spartan saw widespread service in the RAC, with the REME Light Aid Detachments, in armoured infantry battalions, and with the Royal Engineers. It has now largely been replaced by the Panther Command and Liaison Vehicle, based on the LMV made by Iveco and will finally be retired from service with the British Army in 2023. From 2003 Spartan were upgraded to the FV103 Spartan 235 CVR(T) standard and in 2010 39 new CVR(T) Mk 2 hulls were built for service in Afghanistan. While most were fitted with Scimitar turrets, nine saw service as the Spartan Mk 2.

The FV104 Samaritan CVR(T) Armoured Ambulance entered service in 1978 and 50 were built up to 1986. Samaritan is similar to Spartan, apart from the roof being raised by 400mm to create the room necessary for stretchers and medical equipment. On operations, the vehicle is crewed by three men: a driver, a commander, who is also a medic, and a second medic. It served with the regimental headquarters squadrons and squadron headquarters troops of the armoured reconnaissance and armoured regiments of the RAC. It similarly went through the various upgrades of the CVR(T) family during the 1990s and 2000s and in 2010 five Mk 2 hulls were configured as Samaritan Mk 2 CVR(T).

The FV105 Sultan CVR(T) Armoured Command Post entered service at the same time and 291 were built up to 1986. Sultan was designed to replace the FV610 Saracen which had previously been used as a command post at regimental level, with three originally serving in each Armoured Reconnaissance Regiment (Tracked) BAOR. Sultan also served in armoured and armoured infantry regiments, as well as with the Royal Engineers and RAF. Sultan had a crew of three – driver, vehicle commander and radio operator – and accommodated two more soldiers in the rear as well as communications equipment. Further space could be provided by a 6m-long tent extension attached to the rear of the vehicle. Ten Sultan Mk 2 vehicles were built in 2011 for service in Afghanistan.

In 1978 the Army also procured 95 FV106 Samson CVR(T) Armoured Recovery Vehicles, six of which served with the RAF Regiment. Samson was designed to provide armoured recovery for units equipped with the CVR(T) and to this end featured a capstan winch which, with the earth anchor deployed, can recover vehicles up to 18.8 tons in weight. It has no crane as such, but used with the scissors-type draw bar, the winch can be used as a jib crane with a lifting capacity of 454kg. Samson served in the LAD sections of the armoured reconnaissance units and in armoured regiments and armoured infantry battalions that operated CVR(T). Samson too underwent various modifications and upgrades throughout its service career and four Samson Mk 2 were produced for service in Afghanistan.

In 1978 Alvis also demonstrated a prototype of the FV433 Stormer. This was based on a

An FV105 Sultan of 1st The Queen's Dragoon Guards during Exercise Bavarian Charger held in the summer of 2013 at the Grafenwoehr Training Area. (MoD Crown Copyright photograph by Cpl Wes Calder RLC)

lengthened Spartan chassis – necessitating an additional roadwheel – and was equipped with a diesel engine. Stormer was to form the basis of a second-generation of CVR(T). It was not until 1986, however, that the MoD decided to procure Stormer as the platform for the Starstreak High Velocity Missile, a replacement for Rapier surface-to-air missile system. Stormer entered service in 1994 and ten Troop Reconnaissance Vehicle (TRV) and 135 Self-Propelled Starstreak HVM (SS HVM) were procured in total. They continue to serve with one regular and one reserve air defence regiments of the Royal Artillery but are due to be replaced by 2023 with the Army's new Sky Sabre Air Defence System. From 1999 until its withdrawal in 2014, the Stormer chassis also provided the basis for the Shielder Vehicle Launched Scatterable Mine System (VLSMS) which replaced the Bar Mine Laying System in the Royal Engineers. 29 Shielder VLSMS were procured, and it was used by 32 Engineer Regiment during Operation Telic in 2003.

An SP HVM of 12 Air Defence Regiment, Royal Artillery, during Exercise Bavarian Charger in 2013. (MoD Crown Copyright photograph by Cpl Wes Calder RLC)

FV101 SCORPION CVR(T)

The new CVR(T) was accepted into service by the British Army in May 1970 and production started on the following 30 July with an initial order for 275 Scorpion and 288 Scimitar. The first vehicles were completed in 1971 and the initial delivery of Scorpion was made to the Royal Electrical and Mechanical Engineer training establishments in January 1972. In October that year A Squadron, The Blues and Royals (Royal Horse Guards and 1st Dragoons) received the first Scorpion for active duty.

The FV101 Scorpion CVR(T) had a box-shaped hull, where the driver sat, and a two-man (commander and gunner) turret fitted with a 76mm L23A1 main gun. It could fire High Explosive Squash Head (HESH), High Explosive (HE), and Smoke: Illuminating and Canister rounds. Forty rounds could be carried, typically fifteen HESH, twenty HE and five Smoke. The turret was also armed with a 7.92mm L43A1 GPMG, with 2,000 rounds of ammunition for the co-axial armament. The turret was fully traversable with an elevation of 35 degree and a depression of ten degrees. The 76mm main gun was a powerful weapon to be fitted to so small a vehicle and it was usually fired with the turret in an eleven or one o'clock position. The gunner benefitted from a L3A1 Image Intensification passive night sight, a novelty for British AFVs at the time. Communications was originally by the Larkspur radio system, but this was replaced from 1978 by the Clansman VRC system.

Scorpion was protected by aluminium-zinc-magnesium AA7017 alloy armour, which kept the vehicle weight down below the stipulated 17,500 pounds at 7.8 tons. The armour gave adequate protection against 12.7mm heavy machine gun rounds in the frontal arc and against 7.92mm elsewhere, as well as against high-explosive shell splinters. The driver's position was further protected by additional aluminium alloy armour against mines.

Scorpion, like all the CVR(T) family, was originally powered by the Jaguar J.60 4.2-litre, six-cylinder petrol engine which produced up to 265 bhp at 5,000 rpm. It could reach speeds of up to 50mph on the road and across country its 432mm-wide aluminium tracks exerted a ground pressure of only 0.338kg/cm^2, less than that of an average man. It was fitted with a Merrit-Wilson TN15X transmission with a semi-automatic gearbox with seven gears both forwards and back. Originally, a flotation screen, manually erected by the crew, allowed the vehicle to ford rivers and streams at a speed of 3.6mph. This, however, was prone to being damaged by the firing of the main gun and was seldom used as pontoon or Medium Girder Bridges were usually available to cross obstacles. It was also unpopular among crews and sometimes discarded, and in the early 1980s the remaining flotation screens were officially removed from Scorpions in service.

Scorpion and Scimitar were rather rushed into service in 1972 to escape the feared defence cuts imminent after the 1969 Defence Review led by the Labour Secretary of State for Defence, Dennis Healey. This meant that certain parts of the CVR(T)

A Scorpion at speed in the 1970s. Note the flotation screen and the early, smaller headlights. The speed provided by the CVR(T) family transformed the close reconnaissance capability of the British Army. (Richard Stickland)

(above) A somewhat battered Scorpion photographed during Exercise Key Flight in 1989. Note the Chieftain stowage bin fitted to the side of the hull and improvised stowage cages at the sides and the front. (Eckhard Ude)

family of vehicles entered service without sufficient testing. In 1976 a series of modifications and upgrades to the vehicle fleet, known as Operation Bargepole, began at the Alvis works in Coventry. The programme addressed problems identified with the gunner's sight and the gearbox. Most importantly, by the late 1970s it was apparent that the CVR(T)'s aluminium alloy armour was prone to what was known as Stress Corrosion Cracking. This was most apparent in the gun mantlet of Scimitar but affected all CVR(T) to some extent. Research at the MVEE at Chertsey led to Operation Scorepole in 1978, replacing cracked armour with a new alloy configured to MVEE 1318B standard. In all some 600 Post Design Modifications were applied to the CVR(T) before production ceased in 1986.

In 1981 the RAF procured 150 CVR(T) to equip its six Light Armour Squadrons (LAS) of the RAF Regiment. These were designed to protect Harrier airfields in the forward area of 1 (BR) Corps in Germany and elsewhere. Each LAS comprised an HQ and Engineer Flight with one Sultan and one Samson, three Spartan Flights with fifteen Spartans, and a Scorpion Flight comprising six Scorpion. During the 1970s and 80s the British Army's Scorpions received several external changes, mainly to address the lack of storage for the crew's personal gear, but also including some driven by their experience in service. From the late 1970s Scorpion and other CVR(T) began to be fitted with larger seven-inch diameter headlights as a result of the experience of those units serving with the Allied Command Europe (ACE) Mobile Force (Land) in Norway.

Scorpion, as we shall see, served with distinction in the war to liberate Kuwait in 1991, but by then concerns had been raised about the toxicity of the fumes released in the turret when firing both the 76mm gun and the 30mm Rarden cannon of Scimitar. In November 1991 tests at the Gunnery School in Lulworth revealed that levels of hydrogen chloride, hydrogen sulphide and hydrogen cyanide exceeded the Short-Term Exposure Level safety limits. This unfortunate discovery coincided with a major re-evaluation of the United Kingdom's defence needs in the wake of the collapse of the Soviet Union and the end of the Cold War. In 1990 *Options for Change* had seen the manpower of the Army reduced by eighteen per cent to 120,000 personnel and the eighteen regiments of the Royal Armoured Corps reduced to just ten through a series of amalgamations. In the same year the Conventional Armed Forces in Europe (CFE) treaty between NATO and Warsaw Pact set limits on the number of AFVs operated by each side. All AFVs armed with guns more than 75mm in calibre were deemed to be tanks giving both NATO and the Warsaw Pact an excuse to retire obsolete and troublesome 76mm-armed AFVs, like the Soviet PT-76 amphibious reconnaissance vehicle and Scorpion, from active service. In 1991 the RAF had decided to retire their CVR(T) as their role of forward protection of airfields was redundant (although they had played this role in the Gulf earlier that year).

In 1993 Scorpion was officially withdrawn from service with the British Army, although some continued in the OPFOR role at British Army Training Unit, Suffield (BATUS) in Canada, where they were renamed Salamander. In all, 1,241 Scorpion were manufactured by Alvis and, in total, 313 were delivered to the British Army and 25 to the RAF between 1971 and 1986. The remainder were for export.

A Scimitar of 16th/5th The Queen's Royal Lancers, which took over as one of the two armoured reconnaissance regiments of 1 (BR) Corps in October 1974, out on exercise somewhere in Lower Saxony. (Richard Stickland)

FV107 SCIMITAR CVR(T)

Scimitar was basically the same vehicle as Scorpion but fitted with a 30mm Rarden cannon as its main armament instead of the 76mm cannon. It was first issued in the spring of 1974 to 17th/21st Lancers and 14th/20th King's Hussars. These were armoured reconnaissance regiments and Scimitar was tasked with providing direct reconnaissance with troops of Scimitar attached to the individual battlegroups of 1 (BR) Corps.

The 30mm L2A1 Rarden cannon was designed to engage enemy APCs, such as the tracked BMP-1 and wheeled BTR-60, in the close reconnaissance role. The Rarden automatic cannon fires clips of three rounds and armour-piercing, discarding sabot tracer (APDS-T), high explosive incendiary (HE-T), armour-piercing, secondary

From 1973 CVR(T) of the armoured reconnaissance regiment attached to the ACE Mobile Force took part in the annual Exercise Hardfall in Norway. This tested the vehicles and their crews to the limits of their endurance. (Richard Stickland)

effect tracer (APSE-T) and practice tracer (PRAC-T) rounds can be fired. The APDS-T rounds are effective against light armour at ranges up to and beyond 1,000m, while the HE rounds is effective against soft targets up to 2,000m. Up to two clips of three rounds can be loaded and fired at once, with empty cases ejected out of the turret. In total, 165 rounds of 30mm ammunition are carried. Like Scorpion, it is also armed with a co-axial 7.92mm L7A1 GPMG and fitted with smoke dischargers, initially fitted with three, later four launchers on each side of the turret. The commander had a No. 75 Mk 1 optical sight and an AV No. 43 Mk 3 periscope, while the gunner had the AV2 L3A1 night sight as fitted to Scorpion.

(above) In its natural environment: a Scimitar crew pause with their vehicle in the rolling hills typical of the terrain 1 (BR) Corps was expected to defend in the event of a Soviet invasion across the Inner German Border. This vehicle was photographed during Exercise Key Flight in 1989. (Eckhard Ude)

A total of 486 Scimitar were made, with 334 delivered to the British Army between 1974 and 1986. Like Scorpion, it underwent the various Post Design Modifications because of problems with the aluminium alloy armour and other features. It also underwent a series of minor modifications to stowage arrangements, headlights and other details during its service life, before the more extensive changes to the sights and the Life Extension Programme (LEP) introduced during the 1990s.

NATO's cold weather exercises in Norway continued until the end of the Cold War. This ACE Mobile Force Scimitar was photographed during Exercise Cold Winter 87. (US Army photo by Cpl. J.D. Gonzales)

UPGRADING THE SCIMITAR: THE LEP

The so-called 'peace dividend' at the end of the Cold War had, as we have seen, led the British Army to the decision to retire its CVR(T) Scorpions from active service, but the Scimitar and other members of the CVR(T) family would need to soldier on into the 21st century. The necessity of an upgrade to the existing CVR(T) fleet had been apparent for some time but the expectation that the whole family would be replaced by a new series of AFVs had delayed its implementation in the late 1970s. By the mid 1980s the shortcomings of the CVR(T) were well known and

(below) A British Army Scimitar takes part in a training exercise along US Marines and members of 45 Commando, Royal Marines, during the Combined Joint Training Field Exercise (CJTFEX) 1996 at Fort Lejeune, North Carolina, in the USA. (US Marine Corps photo by LCpl RL Kluger Jr)

A Scimitar photographed in Studland Bay, Dorset, in 2004 during a commemoration of Operation Smash, a rehearsal for D-Day in 1944. The vehicle is fitted with the E-SPIRE sights. (Peter Brown)

impacting upon its effectiveness in a significant way. Mechanical problems, especially with the 4.2-litre Jaguar petrol engines, were described as 'chronic' by the armoured reconnaissance regiments of BAOR. In 1985 a Scorpion fitted with the Perkins T6.3544 diesel engine was tested by 13th/18th Royal Hussars in Germany and found to perform admirably. It was estimated that the cost of installing new diesel engines would be £15,500 per vehicle, and a careful analysis of converting the existing fleet to diesel over maintaining the older petrol engine estimated a total saving of some £18 million over the next five years.

Nevertheless, the end of the Cold War, the first Gulf War, and the wider review of British military spending in the new geo-political situation that prevailed in the 1990s meant this planned upgrade never materialised. It was not until 1998 that Alvis plc was eventually awarded a contract worth £32 million to initially upgrade 200 CVR(T) with the Cummins BTA 5.9-litre diesel engine. This Life Extension Programme (LEP) was applied to the Spartan APC, Sultan command vehicle, Samson recovery vehicle, Samaritan ambulance and Striker ATGM vehicle, as well as Scimitar and Sabre. In all the contract provided for 1,107 conversion kits to be supplied by Alvis and fitted at a rate of 25 vehicles per month at both Alvis and the Army Base Repair Organisation (ABRO) at Donnington. The Cummins engine was fitted alongside a modified David Brown Defence TN15E gearbox. This increased the range to 600 miles (870km) and gave a top speed of 50mph (80kph) on roads. The first vehicles fitted with the LEP were delivered in April 1999. The LEP also saw a few other small changes, detailed later in the modelling section of this book, and all CVR(T) that went through the programme had new track, first introduced in 1996, installed.

There were several other changes to the Scimitar throughout the 1990s and early 2000s which maintained the vehicle's survivability and lethality on a fast-evolving battlefield. In 1992, as the British Army prepared to deploy for Operation Grapple as part of the United Nations' Protection Force to Bosnia-Herzegovina and Croatia (UNPROFOR), the Ministry of Defence ordered the French defence company Thales to prepare the Enhanced Sight Periscopic Infra-Red Equipment (E-SPIRE) thermal-imaging package. This included a laser rangefinder, fire control computer and the HIRE thermal-imaging package built by Raytheon Systems. Initially 66 Scimitar were fitted with the E-SPIRE package, and these served as part of the British deployment to the NATO-led Stabilisation Force in Bosnia and Herzegovina (SFOR) in 1996. In 1998 the Ministry of Defence awarded Thales a second contract to upgrade a further 170 Scimitar with the second-generation version of the SPIRE, known as M-SPIRE. This package had an enhanced linear cooling system which made the system quieter and more reliable. Subsequent upgrades included a stabilised version, known as U-SPIRE.

A Scimitar 235 of The Household Cavalry Regiment at British Army Training Unit Suffield (BATUS) in Alberta, Canada, during Exercise Prairie Storm 2015. Note the prominent BGTI sights. (MoD Crown Copyright photograph by Cpl. James McAllister)

A clear photograph taken in 2006 of a Scimitar 235 with the new BGTI sights fitted. (JW de Boer)

UPGRADING THE SCIMITAR: NEW CHALLENGES

The past twenty years have seen exceptional challenges to the CVR(T) family and the British Army as a whole, and a series of further upgrades and modifications have been necessary to maintain the CVR(T) as an effective warfighting machine. The most important upgrade was a new thermal-imaging system, the Battle Group Thermal Imaging (BTGI) programme. In August 2001 the Ministry of Defence signed a contract worth £230 million with Thales to supply new thermal-imaging sights to be installed in 146 CVR(T) Scimitar and 361 FV510 Warrior Infantry Fighting Vehicles. The system comprises a stabilised Gunner's Sighting System, a Commander's Crew Station, a GPS-based Inertial Navigation System (GPS/INS), and a Driver's Display. Using the latest technology, the BGTI system significantly enhances the ability of both vehicles to detect and engage targets. The advanced new thermal imager gives much improved situational awareness at night and in poor visibility, while the eye-safe laser rangefinder, fire control system and INS provide for target locations and own position with increased accuracy. The BGTI was finally accepted into British Army service in March 2005. The BGTI is also integrated with the new Bowman C4I communications equipment, a replacement for the venerable Clansmen radio. The Bowman system was accepted into service in 2004 and fully integrated throughout the British Army by 2008. Vehicles with the LEP, BGTI and Bowman upgrades are known as FV107 Scimitar 235 CVR(T).

While the BGTI and Bowman communications equipment were being trialled, the British Army embarked on two of the most demanding missions in its long history: the war in Afghanistan and the invasion of Iraq. Both placed very specific demands on the CVR(T) fleet, and in particular the Scimitar, which was upgraded and modified as a result of a series of Urgent Operational Requirements. Already, following the experience in the Balkans, it had been recognised that the Scimitar required additional protection against mines and Improvised Explosive Devices (IEDs). The wars in Afghanistan and Iraq only made this need more acute. In 2002 a Mine Blast Protection (MBP) was fitted and from the following year, in preparation for Operation Telic, a further Ballistic Programme (BP) was applied to CVR(T) Scimitar, Spartan and Samson. This involved fitting Kevlar composite armour panels manufactured by the Israeli company Plasan-Sasa to the hull and turret sides designed to enhance the protection offered against shell splinters. From 2004 all CVR(T) deployed as part of Operation Telic received Enhanced Protection Bar Armour (EPBA) designed to protect against RPG-7 attack.

The continued challenge of operating in Afghanistan led to further modifications to Scimitar from 2009. In that year the intolerable temperatures suffered by vehicles crews were addressed by the CVR(T) Environmental Mitigation (EM) package. This involved spot cooling for the gunner and commander and a cooling vest for the driver. The NBC filtration system was also removed and replaced by an air-conditioning system. Other changes addressed the mechanical stresses

A Scimitar 235 fitted with the Plasan-Sasa ballistic protection, mine protection and EPBA package in Afghanistan in 2006. (Carl Schulze)

placed upon the vehicle by operating in Afghanistan. An improved aluminium radiator, new air intake snorkel and filter, transmission heat exchanger and fuel-cooling system, a new clutch, improved TN15E+ gearbox, and engine temperature gauge were all introduced to address the chronic number of breakdowns which severely limited the effectiveness of the CVR(T) in Afghanistan.

Another important change was the introduction of the Remote-Controlled IED Electronics Countermeasure System (RCIED ECM). The idea behind this system is to jam the radio frequencies in the immediate vicinity of the vehicle thus preventing insurgent from remotely detonating IEDs as the CVR(T) passes nearby. Together these modifications led to an increase in weight from 7.8 to eleven tons for Scimitar, necessitating new torsion bars and suspension dampers. This CVR(T) Phase Two Upgrade was unofficially known as Operation Pilton by the various companies involved. In all 102 CVR(T) Scimitar were upgraded to this Theatre Entry Standard (TES) for service. A final modification, introduced in 2012 after two soldiers from 1st The Queen's Dragoon Guards died after their Scimitar had overturned after being hit by a mine, was the Roll Over Protection System (ROPS) fitted to the top of the turret.

A Scimitar 235 of the Light Dragoons in Afghanistan in 2012 during Operation Herrick 16. Note the ROPS above the turret, with the RCIED ECM antenna atop it, fitted after two members of the regiment died when their vehicle hit a mine and overturned. (Carl Schulze)

FV107 CVR(T) SCIMITAR: IN DETAIL

As the longest serving member of the CVR(T) family, the Scimitar has undergone the most obvious changes during its service career. These photos highlight some of the most obvious, all of which are detailed in the modelling guide later in this volume.

1 *A Belgian Scimitar at the Gunfire Museum at Brasschaat, Belgium. Apart from the Belgian smoke launchers, this has features typical of an early Scimitar. (Patrick Winnenpennickx)*

2 *At the other end of its service career, a Scimitar LEP with E-SPIRE sights, Plasan ballistic protection and bar armour photographed in 2006. (JW de Boer)*

ENGINE DECK

3 *Scorpion and Scimitar were first manufactured with this bolted transmission, seen here on the Gunfire Museum's Scimitar. All British Army Scimitar had the bolted transmission initially. (Patrick Winnenpennickx)*

4 *The LEP programme and the installation of the Cummins diesel engine saw the installation of a new engine deck and transmission cover, as seen on this Scimitar 235. (JW de Boer)*

SIGHTS

__5__ Scimitar was originally fitted with the No. 75 Commander's Sight and the L3A1 first-generation image intensification sight next to the main armament. (Patrick Winnepenninckx)

__6__ From the late 1980s Scimitar was upgraded with Enhanced Sight Periscopic Infra-Red Equipment (E-SPIRE) thermal-imaging package. (JW de Boer)

__7__ From 2005 Scimitar was improved again with the installation of the Battle Group Thermal Imaging (BGTI) sights. (JW de Boer)

COMMUNICATIONS EQUIPMENT

__8__ The first CVR(T) to enter service were fitted with Larkspur radios, but from 1976 the Clansman combat radio net system was fitted. (Peter Brown)

__9__ From 2004 the Bowman tactical communications system was introduced but it took several years for it to be fitted all CVR(T) in service. It is distinguishable by the large box on the right-hand turret rear of the Scimitar and a different antenna base. (JW de Boer)

LIGHTS

__10__ Scorpion and Scimitar were initially fitted with 5-inch headlights mounted below the flotation screen support. (Patrick Winnepenninckx)

__11__ From the late 'eighties Scorpion and Scimitar began to be fitted with new 7-inch headlights mounted in guards on top of the flotation screen support. These are retained today, although new style side lights have been installed to clear the stowage also mounted on the support. (JW de Boer)

COLOUR PROFILES BY CLAUDIO FERNANDEZ

1. FV101 Scorpion CVR(T), 17st/21st Lancers, Belize, 1979. This Scorpion was part of the CVR(T) troop of six Scorpion provided by the regiments of the Royal Armoured Corps as part of their commitment to the central American state of Belize, designed to counter any potential Guatemalan aggression. The men of 17st/21st Lancers began their six-month tour of duty in September 1979. The vehicle has the name 'Cassino II', a reference to the regiment's battle honour from the Italian campaign during World War II. It is painted in the IRR (Infra-Red Reflective) 'British Olive Drab' and IRR Black camouflage introduced in the mid 1970s.

2. FV101 Scorpion CVR(T), B Squadron, The Blues and Royals, Operation Corporate, The Falkland Islands, May 1982. Two troops comprising eight CVR(T) – four Scorpion and four Scimitar – sailed to the South Atlantic in 1982 as part of 3 Commando Brigade. It wears the same Green and Black camouflage, now standardised as RR NATO Green BSC 381C No. 285 and Black.

(Eckhard Ude)

3

3. FV107 Scimitar CVR(T), unidentified unit, Exercise Key Flight, Germany, September 1989. This rather battered Scimitar is typical of much of BAOR's CVR(T) fleet by the end of the Cold War. The prominent red square suggests this is part of the 'Orange Forces'.

4

4. FV101 Scorpion CVR(T), Reconnaissance Troop, The Royal Scots Dragoon Guards, Operation Desert Sabre, Iraq, February 1991. British AFVs deployed to Saudi Arabia first with Operation Granby were painted in theatre with a variety of locally available paints, including the official Light Stone BSC 381C No. 361. This vehicle also carries the luminous aerial recognition marker, the inverted chevron applied to all Coalition vehicles, and a Union Flag to avoid any 'blue-on-blue' incidents.

5

5. FV107 Scimitar CVR(T), C Squadron, 1st The Queen's Dragoon Guards, 1st (UK) Armoured Division, Operation Telic, southern Iraq, March 2003. This Scimitar has a partial coat of Light Stone applied over the NATO Green.

6. FV107 Scimitar CVR(T), Reconnaissance Troop, The King's Royal Hussars, KFOR, Macedonia, May 1999. The Scimitar of King's Royal Hussars' Reconnaissance Troop waited in Macedonia for almost two months before they moved into Kosovo in June as part of NATO's Kosovo Force (KFOR). The vehicle wears the standard NATO Green and Black scheme.

6

7

7. FV107 Scimitar CVR(T), C Squadron, The Light Dragoons, UNPROFOR, Operation Grapple, Vitez, Bosnia-Herzegovina, winter 1993. C Squadron, The Light Dragoons deployed to Bosnia in November 1993. As part of the United Nations force the regiment's CVR(T)s were painted white and had 'UN' painted in large black letters on the glacis plate and turret side stowage bins. Some also had UN registration plates as well as their UK ones.

(Carl Schulze)

8. FV107 Scimitar 235 CVR(T), A Squadron, The 9th/12th Royal Lancers (Prince of Wales's), Operation Herrick 14, Gereshk, Afghanistan, summer 2011. This heavily weathered Scimitar is typical of the dirty, dusty vehicles supporting the British Army's effort to battle the Taliban insurgents in Hellmand Province. The Scimitar, as well as the Spartan, Sultan, and Samson, deployed to Afghanistan all had the environmental mitigation (EM), urgent operational requirement (UOR) and theatre entry standard (TES) enhancements.

8

(MoD Crown Copyright photograph by Cpl Mark Webster RLC)

9

9. FV107 Scimitar 235 CVR(T), 5th Battalion, The Rifles Battlegroup, Exercise Prairie Storm 1, British Army Training Unit Suffield (BATUS), Alberta, Canada, May 2016. This Scimitar has the BGTI sights and the Plasan additional armour and is one of the vehicles permanently stationed at BATUS for the field training exercises carried out there.

10. FV101 Scorpion CVR(T), 3rd Division, Nigerian Army, Nigeria, date unknown. The Nigerian Scorpions have a colourful four-colour camouflage scheme consisting of a pale grey-green base with oversprayed squiggles of white, dark green and red brown.

10

11

11. FV101 Scorpion CVR(T), Queen Alexandra's Mounted Rifles, Linton Military Camp, New Zealand, 1980s. New Zealand Scorpions were painted in a four-colour scheme, a modified version of the US Mobility Equipment Research & Design Command (MERDC) colours. The four colours were known as Clay Tint, Sun Brown, Vista White and Black.

12

12. FV101 Scorpion CVR(T), Light Armored Cavalry Troop, Mechanized Infantry Division, Philippine Army, 2014. The handful of remaining Scorpion in Philippine service serve with the Light Armored Cavalry troops of the Mechanized Infantry Division, renamed in 2019 as the Armor (Pambato) Division.

13

13. FV107 Scimitar CVR(T), 3 Parachute Lancers, Belgian Battalion, Operation Restore Hope, Kismayo, Somalia, December 1992. When the US-led multinational force first arrived to restore peace to the troubled East African state, national symbols, such as this Belgian flag, were visible on the vehicles. From June 1993, when the UN took over leadership of the mission, these were removed and replaced with UN markings.

FV101 SCORPION

RECONNAISSANCE TROOP, HQ SQUADRON, THE ROYAL SCOTS DRAGOON GUARDS, 7 ARMOURED BRIGADE, OPERATION DESERT SABRE, KUWAIT, FEBRUARY 1991.

1/35 SCALE
AFVCLUB/SCORPION MINIATURE MODELS
DAVID GRUMMITT

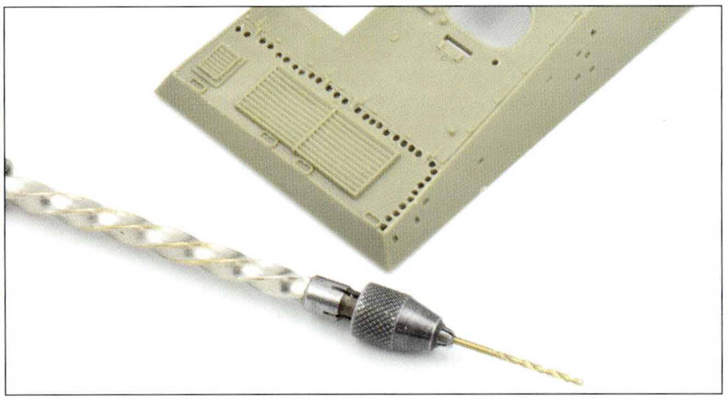

(above) Scorpion Miniature Models' Desert Storm conversion kits are the perfect way to transform AFVClub's kits into Operation Granby vehicles. The first step is to remove the hinged transmission cover from the kit. Begin by drilling small holes around the area to be removed and you can then cut away the unwanted plastic.

(above) Don't remove too much to begin with. Careful sanding and test-fitting is necessary to ensure a good fit for the SMM resin bolted transmission cover.

(below) Probably all Granby Scorpion and Scimitar arrived in Saudi Arabia with the early-style suspension. The SMM conversion set is a perfect fit for the AFVClub lower hull.

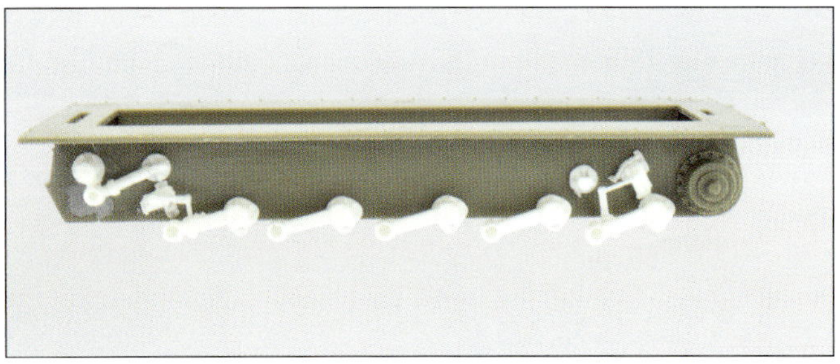

(above) The SMM Operation Granby conversion set also includes an accurately sized and shaped turret, as well as numerous stowage boxes. Even so, almost every CVR(T) in the Gulf had a different arrangement and to model the well-known vehicle from RSDG it was necessary to purchase the Eduard photoetch set (ref. 35347).

(above) The Friul Model tracks are an improvement over the kit ones but are made from very soft metal and are prone to being damaged and breaking.

(above) There was a wide variety of 'sand' shades used to camouflage British AFVs during Operation Granby, but the official colour was Light Stone BSC 381C. I mixed mine from Tamiya acrylics and AK Interactive's Real Color.

(above) The markings for the RSDG Scorpion are contained on the excellent Star Decals set (ref. 35-C1302).

FV107 SCIMITAR

9TH/12TH ROYAL LANCERS (PRINCE OF WALES'S), 4TH (UK) ARMOURED DIVISION, 1 (BR) CORPS, EXERCISE CERTAIN STRIKE, PADERBORN, GERMANY, SEPTEMBER 1991.

1/35 SCALE
AFVCLUB
CHRIS JERRETT

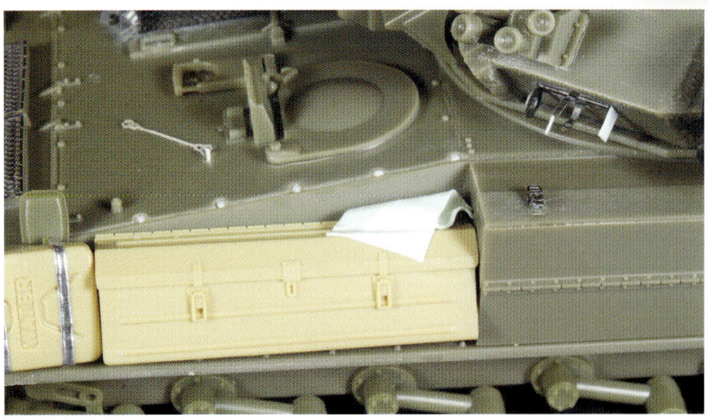

As an out-of-the-box project, AFVClub's Scimitar is straightforward, matching an early nineties Scimitar quite closely. The tan box is from Tamiya's Challenger 1 kit.

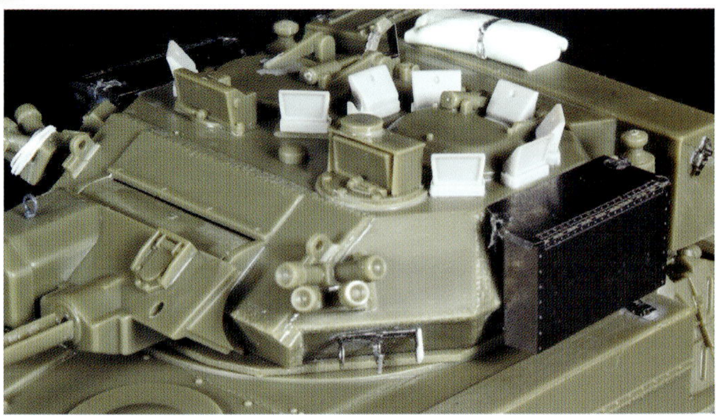

I found Eduard's photoetched set particularly useful when adding the finer details to the model.

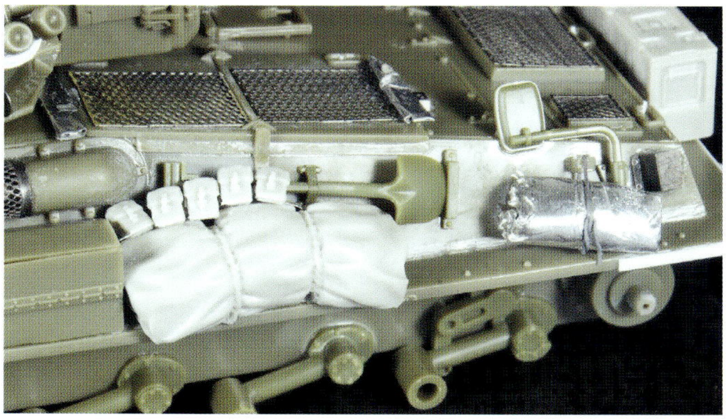

Various pieces of crew equipment were attached to the model, the rolled sheet being a resin item supplied by Legend Productions.

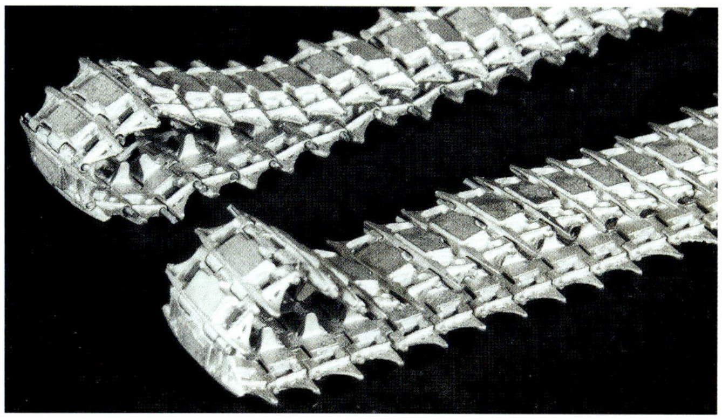

Without doubt, Friulmodel's metal tracks add to the realism, although they can be a challenge to assemble.

A rather pristine BAOR Scimitar waits in the woods somewhere in northern Germany. (Erhard Ude)

It is always a good idea to test-fit the tracks and wheels before applying any paint, as it's much easier to deal with any modifications or repairs at this early stage.

The model was painted with Tamiya acrylics and the markings masked before being airbrushed.

SABRE CVR(T)

2ND ROYAL TANK REGIMENT, 1 MECHANISED BRIGADE, KOSOVO FORCE (KFOR), PRISTINA, 2001.

1/35 SCALE SCORPION MINIATURE MODELS/AFVCLUB

PAUL CROCKER

FEAR NAUGHT

(above) The prominent turret adaptor on the SMM conversion kit, necessary to accommodate the Fox turret in the Scorpion hull.

(above) The SMM conversion for the Sabre is designed to fit the AFVClub Scimitar or Scorpion.

(below) The finished conversion. Note the better-detailed six-spoke resin idlers which are included in the SMM conversion to replace the AFVClub kit parts.

(above) The crispness of the moulding on the SMM Sabre turret is apparent here. Note the Clansmen radio antenna, also from SMM.

(above) The base colours – IRR NATO Green and IRR NATO Black – were laid down using Hataka's lacquer paint.

(above) From the rear you can see the much better-detailed rear hull stowage bin, also included with SMM's Sabre conversion. Note the Friul model tracks and the Eduard photoetched mudguards.

(right) A CVR(T) Sabre stands in a KFOR vehicle park in Multinational Brigade Centre, Pristina, Kosovo in August 2000. Note the highly polished track teeth, hand painted camouflage, and 'Scimitar Hill' written on the hull side bin, a reference to a battle during Gallipoli Campaign in 1915 in which several Yeomanry Regiments served. (Glen Phelan)

FV107 SCIMITAR CVR(T)

A SQUADRON, 9TH/12TH ROYAL LANCERS, 20 ARMOURED BRIGADE,

OPERATION TELIC III, SOUTHERN IRAQ, DECEMBER 2003.

1/35 SCALE
SCORPION MINIATURE MODELS/AFVCLUB
DAVID GRUMMITT

(above) The Scorpion Miniature Models conversion for the Scimitar 235 with Plasan armour is very extensive, using only the roadwheels, drive sprocket, gun barrel and some other small details from the AFVClub kit.

(Carl Schulze)

(above) The photoetch, made by Tetra Model Works, is superb and assembly of the Plasan armour a breeze. It was fixed in position with AMMO's acrylic Ultra Glue, which gives a much longer working time than Superglue.

(above) The finished model: the conversion's BGTI sights were replaced with SMM's E-SPIRE sights, and the supplied Bowman radio replaced with AFVClub's Clansman antenna bases and cable reel.

The MasterClub tracks are superb, if fiddly to assemble. You can see how little of the original AFVClub kit was used in this project.

Vallejo's Russian Green Surface Primer (70.609) served as a good base for the subsequent paint layers and weathering effects.

The Light Stone camouflage was mixed from Tamiya acrylics and applied over a layer of hairspray, allowing me to produce some convincing chipped paint effects.

MODELLING PRODUCTS

Despite its long service and status as one of the most recognisable Cold War British AFVS, the CVR(T) family has attracted relatively little attention from model manufacturers. Nevertheless, it continues to be a popular subject among modellers with new kits and conversions still in the planning and production stage. The aim of this section is to survey the available kits and accessories available and also show modellers how the various kits, conversions, detail sets and accessories can be used to build almost any version of the CVR(T) Scorpion, Scimitar and Sabre.

FULL KITS

The obvious starting point for any discussion of the Scorpion and Scimitar in kit form are the 1/35-scale kits released by AFVClub in 1996. The CVR(T) FV107 Scimitar (ref. AF35013) was very good when it was released and still stands the test of time. It's crisply moulded green plastic sprues, single-piece vinyl tracks, turned metal 30mm Rarden cannon, and small sheet of photoetch allow you to build, out of the box, a more-or-less accurate version of the vehicle as it served with the British Army in the first Gulf War or in the Balkans in the 1990s. That said, the AFVClub does require some modifications and details whatever version you wish to build, and these are detailed in the following section of this book. The corresponding CVR(T) FV101 Scorpion was first released by Revell (ref. 03001) and then in the same year by AFVClub (ref. AF35S-02). This too is an excellent basis for any Scorpion model but, as we shall, will need some corrections and additions to make an accurate model.

The AFVClub/Revell kits were not the first CVR(T) models to be released and in the early 1990s Accurate Armour had released a range of resin, photoetch and white metal kits of various members of the family. These included Alvis Scorpion CVR (ref. K009), a Gulf War 1991 Scimitar (K013DS), FV102 CVR(T) Striker ATGW (ref. K049), FV103 CVR(T) Spartan APC (ref. K0440 and MCT (ref. K045), FV104 CVR(T) Samaritan (ref. K048), CVR(T) Sultan ACV (ref. K046), and FV106 CVR(T) Samson ARV (ref. K047). These kits are still available and, with some experience of working with multi-media, build into nice replicas. There is no doubt though that injection-moulded plastic kits of the rest of the CVR(T) family are long overdue!

A new plastic kit should, however, by available by the time you read this in the form of the Gecko Models FV107 CVR(T) Scimitar Mk 2 TES (ref. 35GM0051). This looks a cracking kit with plastic and photoetch capturing every detail of this relatively new addition to the family. Gecko's kits are often complex and challenging though and this will probably not be one for the beginner.

In the smaller scales, the modeller has slim pickings when wanting to build a CVR(T) variant. Airfix's veteran 1/76-scale Scorpion (ref. 01320) was first released in 1975 and has been reboxed several times over the year, the latest incarnation being in 2005. It represents the vehicle as it entered service in the early 1970s. Alternative parts are included to depict a Scimitar, but it is a very basic model, as you would expect from its vintage. In 2006 Ukrainian manufacturer ACE released 1/72-scale kits of both the FV-101 CVR (Tracked) Scorpion (ref. 72417) and FV-107 Scimitar (ref. 72418). These two kits are a very different proposition to the Airfix one. They represent vehicles from the early to mid 1990s and have some nice details. The tracks, which are made from photoetch, are beautiful but, like the rest of the kit, a little bit of a challenge. Unfortunately, the ACE kits are now out of production and difficult to find. One more kit worth mentioning is the 1/144-scale 3D-printed FV101 Scimitar Vehicle (Scorpion) (ref. HH-14006) by Heavy Hobby. The Chinese company's model looks nicely detailed, but it is, in this scale, extremely small!

CONVERSIONS

Over the years there have been a few conversions designed to make different variants of the Scorpion, Scimitar and Sabre from the basic AFVClub/Revell kits. Most of these

CAD render of Gecko Models 35GM0051

(above) AFVClub AF35013

(above) Revell 03001

(above) Gecko Models 35GM0051

(above) Airfix 01320

(above) Ace 72417

(above) Ace 72418

(above) SMM3525

(above) SMM3526

are now long out of production, including the resin sets produced by Cromwell Models and Castoff in the early 2000s. More recently, however, the modeller has been blessed by the joint efforts of Hong Kong Creation Workshop and Scorpion Miniature Models. The next section of this book shows how their various conversions and detail sets can be used to build most variants of the three CVR(T). One conversion to note here, however, is the Scorpion Miniature Models' Scorpion 90. This is available in three versions – Venezuelan (ref. SMM3526), Malaysian (ref. SMM3525) and Indonesian (ref. SMM3524) – and contains a new resin hull and turret, as well as track guards and other details. Also of note is the very good 3D-printed conversion for the Spanish Scorpion offered by FC Modeltrend. Initially three sets were issued for the Spanish version (refs. 35481, 35568), as well as a set of 3D-printed tracks (ref. 35554), as the Spanish Scorpions were fitted with the same tracks as installed on the CVR(T) Stormer with chevron-shaped trackpads. This set has been superseded by a new set, produced in conjunction with Scorpion Miniature Models, to build a Spanish Marines' vehicle (ref. 35847).

DETAILS SETS

There have been several details sets issued for the AFVClub/Revell kits, both in resin and photoetch. Airwaves, one of the pioneers of photoetched details, offered both a detail set (ref. AFV35076) and a photoetched flotation screen (ref. AFV35092). Eduard, another early frontrunner in the field of photoetch, offered several sets for both the Scorpion and Scimitar (refs. 35186 for the Scorpion, upgraded in 2002 ref. 35457, and ref. 35633 for the Scimitar), as well as a simplified 'Zoom' set (ref. TP104), which included engine deck and exhaust pipe grilles. Other resin detail sets are produced by Scorpion Miniature Models are covered in the next section of this book.

REPLACEMENT TRACKS

One of the weaker areas of the AFVClub/Revell kit are the one-piece vinyl tracks. AFVClub offer plastic individual links sets for both the early (ref. AF35290) and late, post-1996, tracks (ref. AF35294). These are beautifully detailed and should simply click together, remaining workable without any need for glue. The tracks, however, are very fragile and prone to collapsing if not secured with some glue. Friul Model offer white metal individual tracks, both the early type (ref. ATL-106) and the later version (ref. ATL-107). These are also very good, but necessarily small and rather painstaking to drill out and assemble. A third option is Masterclub's Tracks for CVR(T) family (ref. MTL35218). These represent the earlier (pre-1996) style and consist of a metal link, rubber trackpad and tiny resin track pins. These are not for the faint-hearted, but patience and some degree of skill will result in a superb set of workable tracks.

(above) FC Modeltrend 35847

(below) AFVClub AF35294

DECALS

Fortunately, there are plenty of marking options available for modellers of the CVR(T) family. The AFVClub/Revell kits contains markings for Belgian, British and Spanish vehicles in both NATO and UN service. Star Decals produce a number of sets covering the first Gulf War (ref. 35-C1302), service in the Balkans (ref. 35-C1160), and the Scorpion and Scimitar in foreign service (refs. 35-C1201, 35C1202). Bison also produced a set of four markings for the mission in Bosnia (ref. 35006). FC Modeltrend do a nice set of markings for Spanish Marines' Scorpions (ref. 35228). Small-scale sets for New Zealand and Irish vehicles have been released by Oldmodel Decals (refs. OMD1208, OMD2019) and Max Decals (ref. 772) respectively, but these are difficult to find.

(above) Star Decals 35-C 1302

(above) Star Decals 35-C 1201

MODELLING THE CVR(T): FV101 SCORPION

The CVR(T) has had a long service history, spanning five decades, and, as we have seen, the vehicles have undergone a series of changes, modifications and upgrades over that time. The AFVClub/Revell Scorpion, if built straight out of the box, represents a late-production vehicle issued to the RAF Regiment in 1981 or an export version. This means it would not have the flotation screen as this started to be removed in 1980, four-barrel smoke dischargers instead of the earlier three-barrel one, and the hinged transmission cover, instead of the bolted one which most serving Scorpions had.

These are the obvious changes. Another common complaint about the AFVClub/Revell kit are the Messier dampers (horizontal shock absorber assemblies attached to the front and rear road wheel arms) as they were a modification much later in CVR(T) service, around 1990/91. Although the Scorpion was withdrawn in 1993, the question of how many were retrofitted with it remains unclear.

To back-date the Scorpion, Hong Kong Creation Workshop offers a comprehensive set (ref. CK3504), the components of which are also available individually. Starting with the lower chassis, the kit provides both the 'early' idler wheel (C25/C26) and 'late' type (C30/C31), although the instructions only indicate the 'early' type to be used. However, many references show a plain-dished idler wheel (solid with no hole) should be used. The Armstrong damper and bump stops (adapted from a Leyland bus apparently) were used as suspension for most Scorpions. However, the rear bump stops/dampers were removed very early during their service life. The hinged-type transmission cover comes with the kit's upper hull (A4). If you are building a British Army Scorpion, this must be changed and the HKCW set includes the necessary resin replacement. Fibre-glass mudguards and fenders, also included in the back-date set, were installed when it first came into service, but they were easily damaged and were soon discarded.

Moving on to the upper hull, we have the flotation screen. The first 59 were believed to be installed without the tin cover. From the sixtieth vehicle, a sheet metal 'blast guard' was installed across the front and at the sides for the first few feet to stop the blast of the 76mm gun blowing out the skirt. Later, it was completely covered probably to prevent damage to the screen. However, it started to be removed altogether in 1980 as there was no longer a need for wading operations. With the flotation screen raised, there was also a need to have an exhaust extension to direct the exhaust upwards. This is the thick pipe with a right-angled bend on one end stored just underneath the exhaust muffler. With the removal of the screen, this disappeared as well. Below the exhaust extension, there is an aerial stowage case. Later, this was moved to on top of the RHS bin (A5/A18) when installed. This is an omission in the kit.

The exhaust cover in the kit is made of photoetch (G3) to represent the mesh type. Many modellers complain that this is too stiff to work with but placing it over a flame will soften – or anneal – it to bend it more easily. There is obviously the other choice of using other aftermarket photoetch parts, as offered by Eduard (ref. 35457) and, for those interested in backdating it, the early exhaust shroud is solid. The exact time of this switching is uncertain, and some Scorpions were seen with the solid exhaust shroud towards the end of their service, even being carried on to some prototypes of the Sabre.

Another omission in the kit is the stowage of either an axe or sledgehammer on the RHS hull underneath the

(above) CK3504
(below) SMM3512

(above) CK3523
(below) SMM3510

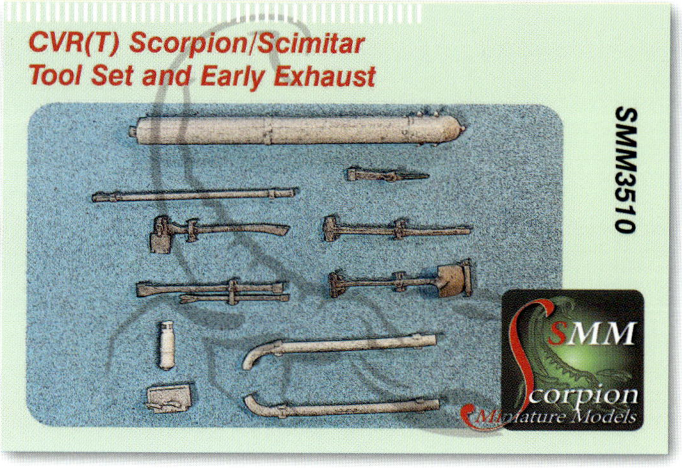

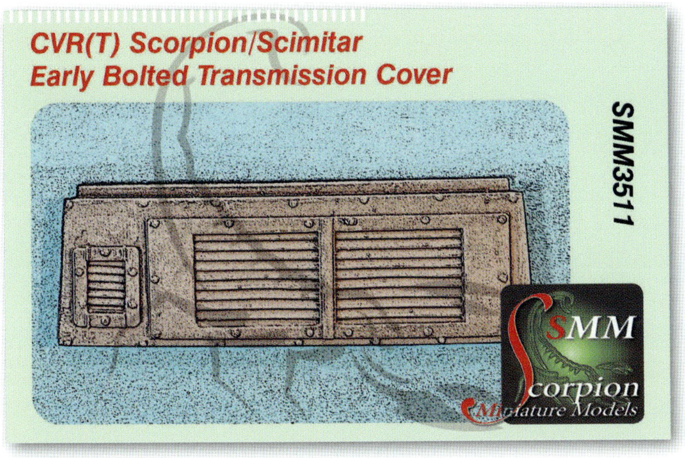

(above) SMM3511

(above) CK3515

shovel. This correct early stowage is also included in the HKCW back-date set. Obviously, the pioneer tools would be relocated if a storage bin was available. The long and thin LHS bin (E14) was standard configuration for the Scorpion, but the shorter and wider one as in the Scimitar kit (F3/F8) became standard after the flotation screen was removed. Even a long stowage bin borrowed from Chieftain was commonly installed after the removal of the flotation screen.

At the rear of the vehicle, there was no rear hull bin when Scorpion entered service. Even the NBC intake (A3) was just a round tubular shape, and the familiar rectangular pipe was soon installed. REME and local workshops fabricated different versions of stowage racks and large suitcases were commonly stored there during exercises. A purpose-built rear hull bin (A1/A6/A7 in the kit) was believed to have been standardised in 1980 (or might be even earlier as its design was detachable to make room for the erection of the flotation screen which had begun to be removed by then!)

Finally, there are the headlights. Smaller 5" lights were originally mounted below the flotation screen platform. With the removal of the latter, sometimes they were moved to the upper surface of the platform. During the last stage of its service, late 80s to early 90s, larger 7" headlights (F7 from Scimitar kit) were mounted with or without a shroud. Sometimes the shroud could be seen with no headlights inside, but the old headlights still under the platform!!

The AFVClub/Revell turret is the wrong size and shape and HKCW produce a resin replacement (ref. CK3523), while there is a separate Scorpion Miniature Models detail set (ref. SMM3512) for the early turret details. Sticking with the kit turret, it was not just the Spanish Scorpion that was not fitted with the thermal intensifier (E1/E16/E17). Even the British Scorpions did not have it installed at the very beginning of its service life. It is also worth noting that in the original instructions (on first release, now corrected in more recent kits), E17 was mistakenly marked as E18. The four-barrel smoke dischargers were only fitted to late-production RAF Scorpions and those versions exported. The majority of British Army Scorpions were installed with the three-barrel smoke dischargers up until the turret was withdrawn from service. Stowage was always an issue after it came into service. However, the turret rear bin (E8/E9/E12/E13) that comes with the kit was installed at a very early stage. Make sure you do NOT drill holes on both sides (E12/E13) as indicated in the instructions. These are to attach the two Chieftain boxes (G) which were a later unofficial modification. Various attachments, such as the cable reel (F), jerry can and even a large fire extinguisher, were seen, so check your references.

The small fire extinguishers (C21) were seen in various places and different positions on the turret, in particular the position at the left lower frontal face of the turret, as indicated in the instructions. The fire extinguisher (D8) attached to the LHS of the hull should be the BCF type at the beginning as well. There was an open-topped first-aid kit holder installed in this position at the very beginning and the kit was probably relocated inside the vehicle later.

The left-hand side of the turret seems to be quite empty but, in fact, there was a PVC hold-all issued as stowage. However, it was very flimsy and always tore apart when running in the field. Later, all sorts of ammunition boxes (81mm mortar boxes seemed to be the crews' favourite) and other bins were bolted to its aluminium structure. Welding onto aluminium was impossible.

HKCW and Scorpion Miniature Models also produce sets for a Falklands War Scorpion and Scimitar (ref. CK3515), which need to be combined with the relevant back-date set. The CVR(T) sent to the South Atlantic all had the old suspension and bolted transmission cover, but the flotation screens had been removed. The square turret rear bin and the removable hull rear bin were fitted, while a jerry can was carried on the left-hand side of the turret bin. There are no clear photos showing the sprocket and idler wheels, but the early type sprockets (C23/C24) and plain solid (not spoked) idler wheels were probably used.

A very specific Falkland modification was the installation of a transmission breather cowl to which was attached a flexible hose that ran along the right-hand side of the hull. They believed they might have to 'swim' ashore. The hose soon disappeared once they landed, but the breather cowl stayed on until the end of the conflict. There was also a large fire-extinguisher carried on the right of the turret rear bin, in addition to a second left-hand side hull bin. 81mm mortar stowage boxes, Rarden 30mm ammunition boxes, and spare road wheels and/or sprocket rings were seen carried around the vehicle, either on the front deck (sprocket rings), or under or on the sides of the rear hull bin. Each vehicle was a little different, however, so check your references. The general rule for Scorpion was that no stowage boxes were carried across the front, as the blast of the 76mm gun would blow them open! There is one photo taken on Ascension Island, where they performed live-fire drills, with Scorpions with mortar boxes across the front and this is probably where they learnt their mistake.

HKCW also produce a conversion set for an Operation Granby Scorpion (ref. CK3547). Most CVR(T) had 'RAF Regiment' turret bins on both turret sides and the rear by this time, and the rear turret bin was the wider and

(above) CK3547

(above) SMM3548
(below) SMM3514

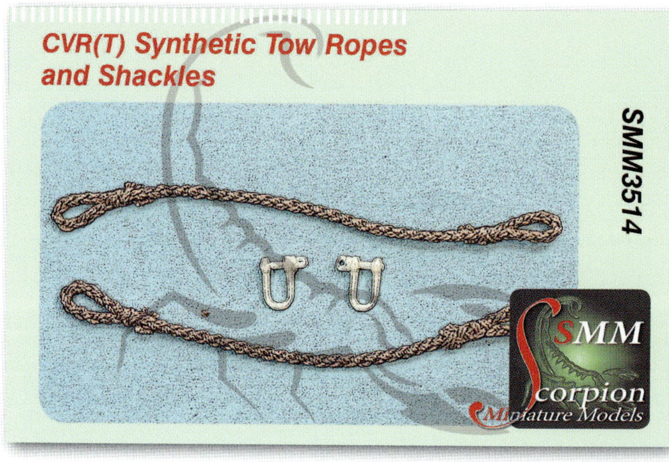

angled type for carrying the OTIS thermal sight. On the right side of the rear bin (sometimes both sides) was a Chieftain grease gun bin. Without the 'RAF' bins fitted on the sides, Chieftain grease gun bins or large ammunition boxes could also be seen on Scorpions. An OTIS ring mount was standard on top of the commander's periscope. Extra smoke grenade boxes appeared at various locations around the turret.

On the hull, the rear boot bin remained the same. The left-side hull box (driver's bin) was wider and deeper, thanks to the removal of the flotation screens, a feature probably introduced at the same time as the 'RAF' turret bins. In front of the driver's bin was a half-length Chieftain tool bin fitted under the driver's hatch and bolted onto the sponson. Welding was impossible due to the aluminium construction of the vehicle. The right side of the hull had a second half Chieftain tool bin bolted onto the track guard in front of the exhaust. The hull front had a half-length Chieftain bin, made shallower by cutting it just below the centre pressed rib, with a new bottom welded in place so it sat in line with the top of the hull front. 7.62mm ammo boxes were bolted either side of the Chieftain bin. Jerrycans were bolted to the ends of the boot bin, some vertical, some angled, in a variety of different frame styles (two styles of frame are included in the HKCW set). A shovel was usually carried on the boot bin. Scorpion Miniature Models also produce an additional Gulf War Stowage set (ref. SMM3548).

Scorpions remained in service until 1993. Towards the end of their service, you will find a large left-hand side bin on the hull (F3/F8 from Scimitar kit), along with a jerry can (F22*, only included in the Scimitar kit) and turret side bins (F2/F13/F17 and F4/F14/F16*) appearing on both sides. The angled rear turret bin (F1/F7/F19/F20*) appeared at the same time as the OTIS (Observer's Thermal Imaging System) sight mount (the circle on top of the commander's periscope (F12*). In fact, this should be a ring with two wing nuts on the rear face to fasten the sight. The sight was only used when the vehicle was static and was stored in the rear turret bin. The later spoked idler (C30 and C31) was fitted, and the Messier dampers as supplied in the kit were, as mentioned above, a late modification introduced around 1990/91. Interestingly, the bolted transmission cover and those three-barrel smoke dischargers remained unchanged until the Scorpion retired from British service.

Shackles and tow ropes (ref. SMM3514) were a common sight stored on CVR(T) instead of steel tow cables. In many publications the tow ropes are called Kinetic ropes. Strictly speaking this is incorrect. A pair of 8' polyester ropes were carried by CVR(T)s and the Kinetic rope (which was 30 foot long) was supplied one per troop or as standard equipment in Samson. The Kinetic rope would be attached to the vehicle ropes and used for recovery.

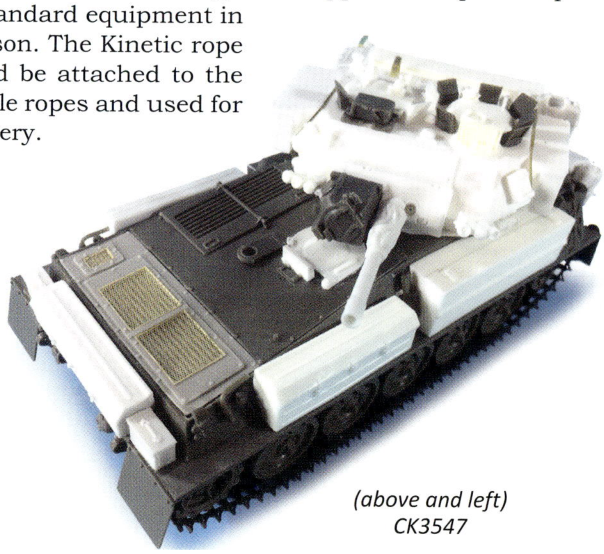

(above and left) CK3547

(above) CK3505

(above) SMM3513

MODELLING THE CVR(T): FV107 SCIMITAR

AFVClub/Revell's Scimitar is basically the same kit as their Scorpion and only Sprue E from the Scorpion kit was replaced by Sprue F in the Scimitar kit, consisting of the gun mantlet and turret boxes. The Scimitar also includes the shorter and wider bin on the left-hand side of the hull and the water jerrycan behind it, while the larger 7" headlights are included, but without any shrouds around them. Built out-of-the-box, you are going to have a mid-service Scimitar, as seen during Operation Granby and the deployment to the former Yugoslavia in the 1990s.

Once again HKCW have a set to backdate the Scimitar (ref. CK3505), the components of which are also marketed separately under the Scorpion Miniature Models label. These include the bolted transmission cover (ref. SMM3511) and fibre-glass mudguards (included in SMM3507). Finally, you should replace the more modern Messier dampers with the old suspension system on the lower chassis (ref. SMM3509). The flotation screen on the upper hull (ref. SMM3507) was slightly different to the Scorpion as it did not have the thin metal cover around the front quarters (so the whole screen was uncovered), as the Scimitar would not blow out the flotation skirt when firing the 30mm cannon! In any case, these screens started to be removed from the late 1970s and permanently discontinued in the early 1980s. The exhaust extension, solid cover over the exhaust, aerial stowage case, exhaust cover, sledge hammer/axe – all included in the early exhaust and tool set (ref. SMM3510) – small headlights, and stowage bins all more or less follow the same path as the Scorpion.

The turret is different proposition, however. When Scimitar first entered service, or during the very early stages of its service life, there was no OTIS sight in use, so a few changes are needed. The OTIS mount on top of the commander's sight (the circular object) must be removed, as well as the larger rear turret bin (AFVClub kit numbers F1, F7, F19 & F20). Without OTIS fitted, this must be changed back to the original rectangular bin (E8, E9, E12 & E13) as used by Scorpion. OTIS was introduced from December 1988. There also should not be any turret side bins. Originally very early crude PVC holdalls and ammunition boxes were in use. Four-barrel smoke dischargers seem to have been used from the start on Scimitar (ref. SMM3513). In addition, an extra smoke launcher box (B1) and additional storage box (E10) were fixed to the right-hand side of the turret.

Many modellers complained that the barrel sleeve on the 30mm Rarden cannon was rarely seen without a cover, so a simple canvas must be added to hide/protect the barrel inside the barrel sleeve in most cases. A canvas cover over the muzzle was also very common, both of which are contained in the early Scimitar turret detail set (ref. SMM3513). Another general improvement to the AFVClub kit – both the Scorpion and Scimitar – is to remove the overly thick track guards and replace them with photoetch guards (ref. SMM3516 which also includes mudflaps and reflectors). An early Scimitar, after stripping off those extra storage bins and with an almost completely different lower hull with screens, bolted transmission cover and early suspension, looks quite different to one built out of the box from the AFVClub kit.

The modifications needed for a Falklands War Scimitar, contained in the HKCW conversion set, have largely been covered under the Scorpion, with the exception that Scimitar could carry 120mm/Trip Flare (C238 Mk.2) boxes (commonly mislabelled as 81mm mortar ammunition boxes) across the front. As with the flotation

CK3545 Gulf War Scimitar

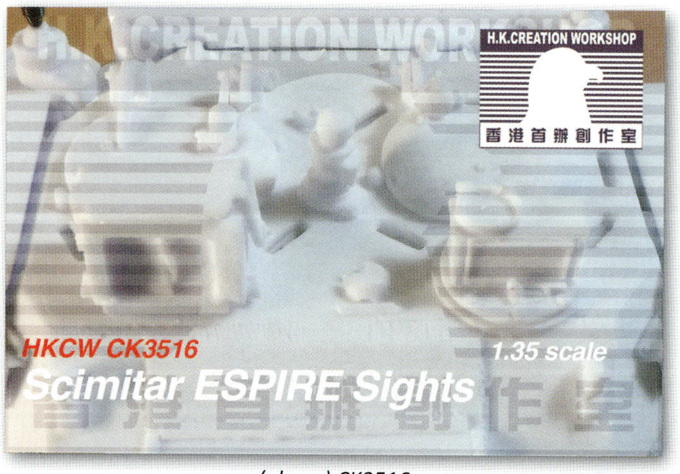

(above) CK3516
(below) CK3517

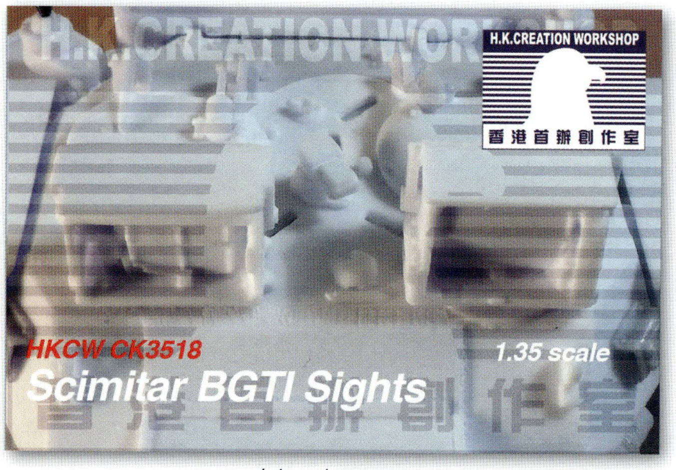

(above) CK3518
(below) CK3522

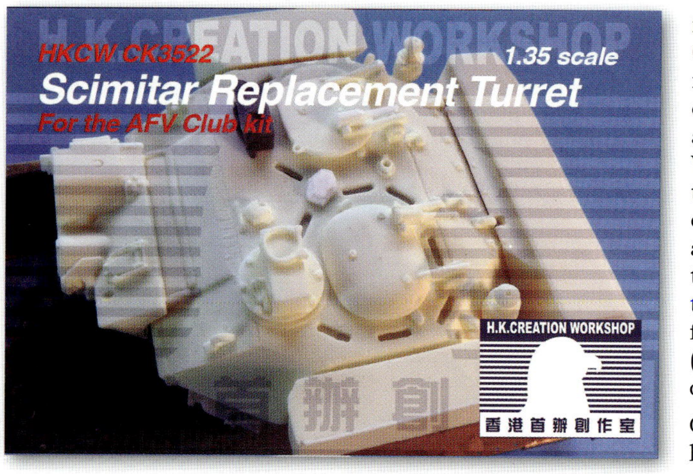

screens, the smaller 30mm Rarden did not affect these boxes across the front, unlike the larger gun on Scorpion which tended to rip them open. A large fire extinguisher, a water jerry can, and a cable reel were also carried on the rear turret bin, so check your references on which particular vehicle you are modelling for the placement of various storage and at which stage of the conflict, such as the transmission breather cowl, which was kept until the end, though the pipe had been removed at a very early stage. Very common on Falkland CVR(T)s during the campaign were the synthetic recovery ropes (ref. SMM3514).

By 1990 and the first Gulf War, the Scimitar had been fitted with OTIS (Optical and Thermal Sights), while all sort of storage bins, standard or otherwise, also found their way onto the vehicle. Even Chieftain bins (F5, F25, F26 and C2, C3, C4, C5, C6), as well as the turret side bins (F2, F13, F17 and F4, F14, F16) are included in the AFVClub Scimitar kit. The OTIS mount (F11) together, with a new rear turret bin (F1, F7, F19, F20) specially designed to house this bulky optic, became standard equipment for Scimitar just before the outbreak of the Gulf War. The Messier dampers (as in the kit) were also beginning to be installed on Scimitar (introduced from September 1990 onwards), though the older Armstrong suspension remained in large numbers as well. However, no two Scimitars were the same, so check references for any particular vehicle. The AFVClub kit provides you with everything to build a Scimitar in the 1990s, including the later hinged transmission cover. With some good references, and maybe some photoetched detail sets, you can build many different vehicles from this period.

In 1998 the E-SPIRE (Enhanced Sight Periscopic Infra-Red Equipment) was introduced for the Gunner. These are available as resin replacements from HKCW (ref. CK3516). It has a new large sight for the gunner (right side) with a moveable protective shutter. The commander kept the normal sight with the OTIS mount still retained, although it was no longer in use at this point. These vehicles also featured TNTLS (Tactical Navigation & Target Locating system). This features a sprung GPS mast fitted to the hull left rear track guard, while a GPS antenna (PLGR - Precision Lightweight GPS Receiver) was fitted to the turret roof between the commander's and gunner's hatches. A Driver's GPS Repeater Display was slightly right and in front of the driver's hatch (but not fitted to all vehicles). ESPIRE was originally fitted to petrol-engined vehicles with Clansman radio (for example, those serving in Bosnia with IFOR, 1995-96). Clansman radio was still fitted to vehicles after the LEP upgrade. In 1996 new tracks were also introduced, produced as the late-pattern track by AFVClub.

The LEP (Life Extension Programme) of the early 2000s is covered by HKCW's LEP Hull Conversion set (ref. CK3517). The LEP upgrade saw the Jaguar petrol engine replaced by the Cummins diesel engine. This involved changing the configuration of the engine deck grilles and adding an air intake to the right side of the hull front. Various stowage bins from Sabre were installed during the LEP, except for the sloped right-hand hull bin which conflicted with the position of the new diesel engine's air intake. These bins included three small bins across the front of the hull and a LHS bin which was flush with the top of the engine deck. With the purpose-built hull front bins, the original vertical direction indicator lights (which would have been hidden behind the new bins) changed to a horizontal arrangement.

Other modifications included a new barrel clamp on the hull front; a larger rear hull bin which had an external

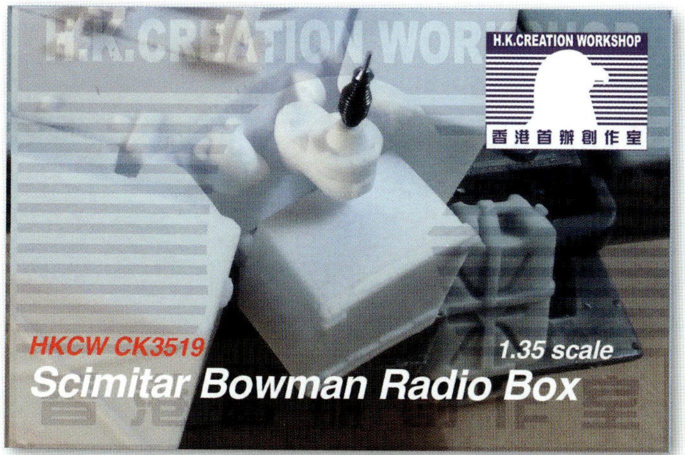

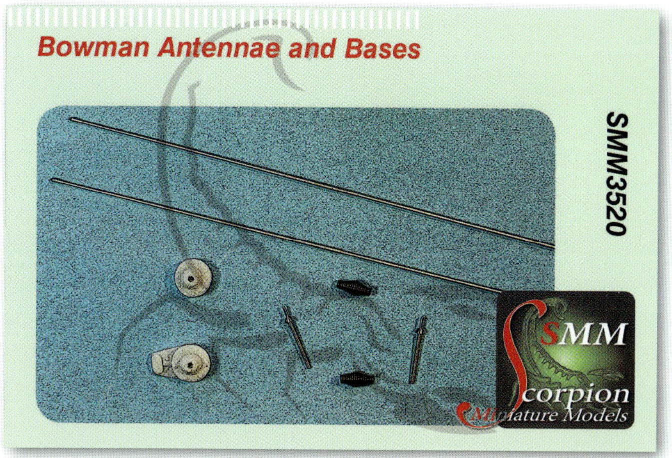

(above) CK3519
(below) SMM3529

(above) SMM3520
(below) CK3530

CK3530

frame (the previous smaller bin had smooth outer walls); a larger diameter exhaust pipe (the protective screen stayed the same); shrouds for the larger headlights; and a new type of Fire Extinguisher (Foam), which was cream in colour. The Bowman radio replaced the previous Clansman system from 2004. This was installed in a box at the RHS rear corner of the turret (ref. CK3519, which includes turned brass masts), probably because of a lack of interior space in the turret. The introduction of GPS was part of this upgrade. Bowman radio antennae mounts (ref. SMM3520, also including masts) replaced the previous Clansman antennae mounts.

In preparation for and during Operation Telic the Scimitar underwent a series of further changes. This included Appliqué Armour/Under Belly Mine protection Armour (ref. SMM3529), Cheek armour for the turret, AND Plasan-Sasa perforated armour in 2003 on the hull and turret sides and across the upper front hull. These are all included in the HKCW resin kit (ref. CK2530), which includes resin, photoetch and some parts from the AFVClub kit. Scimitar in Iraq also received EPBA (Enhanced Protection Bar Armour) in 2004, ECM and BGTI (Battle Group Thermal Imaging). The latter is also available separately (ref. CK3518). Unfortunately, to date the bar armour fitted from 2004 is not available as an aftermarket accessory.

MODELLING THE CVR(T): SABRE

The CVR(T) Sabre involved fitting the 30mm Rarden cannon-armed turret from the Fox wheeled armoured car to the hulls of retired Scorpions. Starting with the chassis, Sabre's distinguishing features included extra hull and turret stowage bins. Sabre was among the first CVR(T)s to have standardised additional stowage bins, including one on each side of the hull at the front, sloped to fit the angle of the front deck plate. Sabre never went through the LEP programme, so the air intake for the new engine associated with LEP Scimitar was not needed. Therefore, the right-hand side front bin was a Sabre-only fitting. It had three small bins fitted on the front track guard, either side and between the two large headlights with shrouds. This meant a change to the side indicator light clusters in horizontal cases so the lights could be seen above these bins. A large rear hull bin was also fitted.

Sabre used the bolted transmission cover as per the original Scorpion hull as found in service photos. However, hinged covers were occasionally seen, as the final-production Scorpions for the RAF Regiment had these fitted. Suspension was mainly the newer Messier dampers, as included in the AFVClub kits, as it made sense to choose hulls with new components for the Sabre. The sprockets varied from the 'late' ones supplied in the kit, or even later six-spoked sprockets as used in the LEP programme. The turret required more extensive changes, including an adapter turret ring needed to fit the Fox turret. Extra turret bins were fitted to the turret sides which were much smaller and square looking compared to those fitted to the Scimitar. The way they were attached was quite different, too, given the shape of the turret. The large rectangular bin for OTIS was fitted at the rear of the turret. On top of the turret, the commander's sight had the OTIS mounting ring, while the gunner's sight was like Scimitar, for obvious reasons, some fitted with rubber sun shields. In addition, the same domed commander's hatch was also installed for the gunner to improve his headroom. In-service photos also show some Sabres fitted with the ESPIRE gunner's sights, obviously a later modification, notably in photos on peace-keeping duties with IFOR and SFOR. Scorpion Miniature Models do an extensive conversion for the AFVClub kit (ref. SMM3528), which includes a Fox turret with the Sabre-specific stowage bins, adaptor ring, bolted transmission cover, and choice of idler wheels.

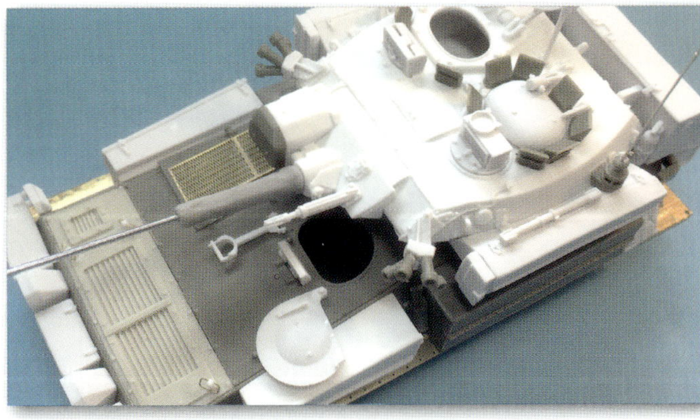

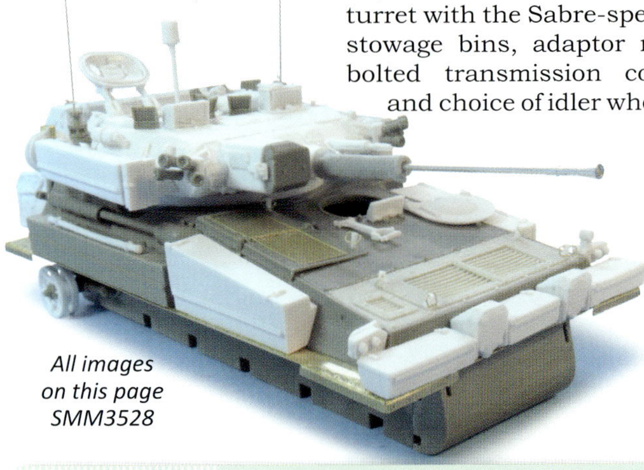

All images on this page SMM3528

2

Parts List

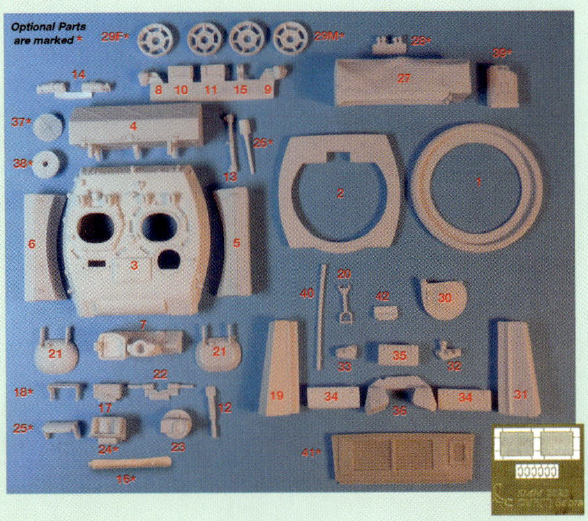

1 Turret ring adapter collar
2 Turret base plate
3 Turret body
4 Rear stowage bin
5 Left side stowage bin
6 Right side stowage bin
7 Gun mantlet
8 Smoke discharger mount, left,
9 Smoke discharger mount, right,
10 Smoke discharger ammunition box, left
11 Smoke discharger ammunition box, right
12 7.62 mm chain-gun barrel
13 Spare chain-gun barrel
14 Fire extinguishers (2 supplied)
15 Cable drum mounting bracket
16 Gun cover * (alternative to kit)
17 Gunner's sight
18 Gunner's sight sunshade *
19 Right-side front stowage bin
20 Extended gun travel lock
21 Domed commander's hatches (2 supplied)
22 Hatch dampers (2 supplied)
23 Commander's sight
24 Gunner's ESPIRE sight head *
25 Gunner's ESPIRE hinged shield *
26 Convoy beacon *
27 Hull rear stowage box
28 'Strongback' mounting brackets (2 supplied) *
29M 6-spoke idlers male (alternative to kit idlers) (2 supplied) *
29F 6-spoke idlers female (alternative to kit idlers) (2 supplied) *
30 Driver's hatch
31 Hull tool box left side
32 Left indicator cluster
33 Right indicator cluster
34 Front stow boxes large (2 supplied)
35 Front stow box small
36 Covered headlights (2 supplied)
37 Cable reel front *
38 Cable reel back *
39 Fuel jerrican* (alternative to kit water jerrican)
40 Antenna tube
41 Bolted transmission cover *
42 Driver's periscope with wiper

PE parts

Engine grille mesh covers
Engine deck cover loops

1

CVR(T) Sabre Conversion SMM3528

This is a conversion set to model the Sabre, based on the *AFV Club* kit.

Sabre was a hybrid vehicle introduced as a less expensive way of producing a similar vehicle to the FV107 Scimitar. It entered service in 1995. This was achieved by combining surplus Scorpion hulls and Fox turrets (both vehicles having been retired by this time) which had the same 30 mm Rarden gun as the Scimitar. As the turret ring diameters were different, an adapter collar was needed negating the Fox turret's lower-silhouette advantage. Some 136 saw service according to official sources of the British Army. It performed peace-keeping missions in the former Yugoslavia with IFOR and KFOR and possibly saw limited service during the Iraq War in 2003. The marriage of the Fox turret and Scorpion chassis was not particularly successful, and Sabre was withdrawn from British Army service in 2004.

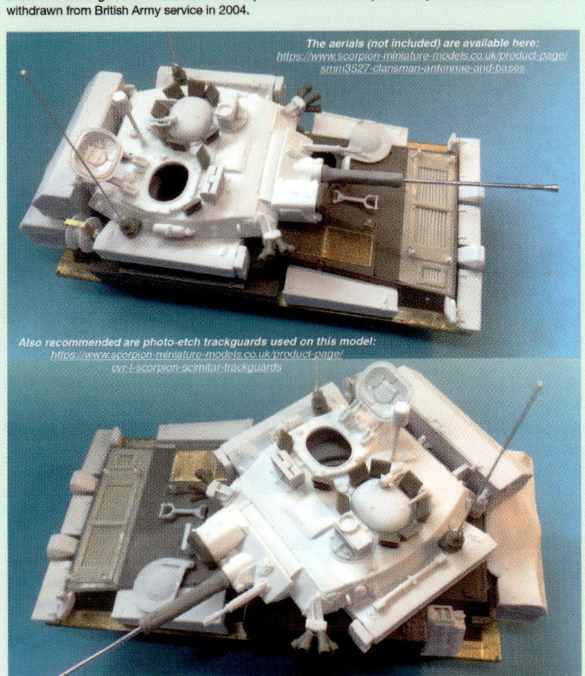

The Light Dragoons deployed to Afghanistan in the summer of 2012 as part of Operation Herrick 16. Here a Scimitar Mk 2 of the Light Dragoons takes part in training at Lulworth in preparation for their deployment to Helmand. (MoD Crown Copyright)

SCIMITAR CVR(T) MK 2

In 2010 the rapidly changing nature of the threat in Afghanistan necessitated a further UOR and led to the Ministry of Defence commissioning a further improvement of the Scimitar's survivability. BAE Systems' CVR(T) modernisation and 'capability shift' programme offered to 'extend, improve and transform' the venerable vehicle for all its users, including the British Army. The Scimitar Mk 2 programme for the British Army was, however, by the far the most extensive, resulting in a very different AFVto that which entered service in the early 1970s. The Mk 2 involved combining the redesigned hull of the FV103 Spartan, with new aluminium armour, with the turret of the Scimitar. The roomier hull of the Spartan allowed for enhanced mine protection measures, which included mine-protected seating for all three crewmen. The programme included a 'dieselisation package', fitting the Cummins 6BTA 5.9-litre engine and coupling this with a new David Brown TN15+ gearbox. Alongside these changes, the Scimitar Mk 2 received an

A clear view of a Scimitar Mk 2, taken at the Tank Museum's 'Tankfest' in 2013, shows the increased height and the TES ROPS and bar armour. (JW de Boer)

A rear view of a Scimitar Mk 2 entering the arena at Tankfest in 2013. (JW de Boer)

improved braking system and suspension dampers, a new radiator and air filters, improved blast protection for the fuel tanks, an air-conditioning system, repositioned foot controls, Thales M-SPIRE FCM, laser-rangefinder and sights, and driver's night-vision equipment. The upgrades increased the weight of the vehicle to 12,500kg, while the new engine delivered 235bhp, providing 33 per cent extra torque. The vehicles' survivability was also enhanced by the new ceramic armour, Enhanced Bar Protection Armour, and a Remotely Controlled Improvised Explosive Device Electronic Counter-Measures (RCIED ECM) system. Some of the Scimitar Mk 2 were also fitted with a Roll-Over Protection System (ROPS) on top of the turret, designed to protect the crew in the event of a roll-over. In all thirty Scimitars, nine Spartans, five Samaritans, ten Sultans and four Samsons were converted to the new Mk 2 standard at a cost of £30,000,000. The new CVR(T) was first displayed at the London DSEi defence and security show in September 2011 and the first deliveries were made to the 9th/12th Royal Lancers serving in Helmand Province, Afghanistan with 3 Commando Brigade shortly afterwards as part of Operation Herrick 14. All the contracted vehicles had been delivered to the Army by the first quarter of 2012. The Scimitar Mk 2 continues to serve with the British Army, but the Theatre Entry Standard (TES) equipment of the bar armour and ROPS is removed for service as part of NATO's Enhanced Forward Presence (eFP) in Poland and the Baltic States.

A Scimitar Mk 2 leads FV510 Warriors on patrol during Exercise Winter Camp as part of the 5 RIFLES battlegroup in Estonia in January 2021. (MoD Crown Copyright)

A CVR(T) Sabre of 1st Royal Tank Regiment attached to the Land Warfare Component Battle Group of the School of Infantry in Warminster, photographed in 2002. Note the distinctive NATO Green and Stone camouflage and the 'Chinese Eye' insignia on the side turret bin. (JW de Boer)

CVR(T) SABRE

In 1993, as we have seen, the 76mm-armed CVR(T) Scorpion was withdrawn from service with the British Army. At that time, the Yeomanry reconnaissance regiments of the Territorial Army were equipped with the FV721 Fox CVR(W). This four-wheeled armoured reconnaissance vehicle was armed with a 30mm Rarden cannon in a turret like that of the Scimitar. It was decided to mate the turrets of the retired Foxes with the hulls of the similarly redundant Scorpions. The work was carried by 34 Base Workshop REME in Donnington using conversion kits supplied by Alvis. The two prototypes were extensively tested at the Armoured Trials and Development Unit (ATDU) at Bovington Camp in Dorset before the Sabre was accepted into service in August 1993.

The installation of the Fox turret onto the Scorpion hull was not straightforward, as the two had different turret ring sizes, and Alvis supplied a special armoured collar that sat on the Scorpion hull to accommodate the turret. The collar meant that the turret sat higher on the Sabre than it had done on either the Fox or the Scimitar. There were several other modifications made to the Sabre from the baseline Scorpion and

(below) A close-up of another 1 RTR Sabre on Salisbury Plain in 2002. Note the prominent flash suppressor of the Chain Gun, the reconfigured smoke grenade launchers, and the turret ring adaptor. (JW de Boer)

(above) A unique CVR(T) variant is this Belgian Driver Trainer vehicle. Only Belgium used this for their aspiring CVR(T) drivers, mounting a British Leyland-made cab on a redundant Scorpion hull. They were used at the Panzercavalerie School at Stockem, close to the Luxembourg border. This example is preserved at the Gunfire Museum at Brasschaat. (JW de Boer)

Fox. The co-axial 7.62mm L37 MG was replaced with a 7.62mm Chain Gun with a much larger flash suppressor. This is a prominent identification feature of a Sabre compared to Scimitar when viewed from any forward angle. Smoke discharger mounts were redesigned from those fitted to Fox, extending sideways from the upper turret wall and comprising four 66mm launch tubes on each side of the turret. The commander's and gunner's hatches were also raised to give more head room when operating with the vehicle closed up.

A total of 138 Scorpion hulls were converted to Sabre at 34 Base Workshop and they remained in service until 2004 when the decision was taken not to convert it to the Cummins diesel engine then being fitted to Scimitar. The Sabre was issued to the reconnaissance platoons of the Mechanised Infantry regiments, as well as the Household Cavalry Regiment, the Queen's Own Yeomanry (a Territorial Army unit), and 24 Airmobile Brigade (later 16 Air Assault Brigade). The Sabre served alongside other members of the CVR(T) family during the British Army's operations in Bosnia and Kosovo.

(below) The trainee sits in the usual driver's position of the CVR(T) Driver Trainer, while the cab contains two sets, one for a second trainee and one, with an additional set of controls, for the instructor. (JW de Boer)

CVR(T) IN FOREIGN SERVICE

Just over a year after being accepted for service with the British Army, in June 1971, the Belgium government signed a contract with Alvis for 701 CVR(T)s of various sorts. After the United Kingdom, Belgium was the most important user of the Scorpion and Scimitar with 133 of the former and 153 of the latter being delivered by November 1980 when all seven contracts for the supply of CVR(T) had been fulfilled. Belgium's decision to acquire the CVR(T) to replace its fleet of Willy Jeeps and M41 light tanks was largely determined by the need for an air-portable system to defend Belgium's last remaining colonial territories in central Africa and by the concession that the vehicles could be assembled by the British Leyland plant in Malines. The Belgians deployed all members of the CVR(T) family between 1971 and their final withdrawal from service in 2004. The CVR(T) served with three cavalry regiments, the Paracommando Regiment Reconnaissance Squadron, and the Armoured Cavalry and Reconnaissance schools. The story of the Scorpion's and Scimitar's service with the Belgian Army was not without its problems. The communications equipment was initially the US AN/VRC 20-21-22 FM sets, but from 1992 these were replaced with Belgian SAIT and later BAMS sets. All Belgian CVR(T)s were fitted with the unpopular flotation screens during the Cold War, but these were removed in the early 1990s. At the end of the Cold War Belgian drastically reduced its military forces and in 1992 Scorpion and Striker were withdrawn from service, the latter being replaced with a MILAN ATGM fitted to the Spartan APC. Ironically, as the Cold War ended, the Belgium CVR(T) were called upon for

(above) A rare sight: a white-washed Scorpion. This Belgian Scorpion was photographed at Elsenborn Camp near Butgenbach in the winter of 1988. (Belgian Armed Forces Archives via Christian Bray)

(below) A well-laden and camouflaged Belgian Scimitar of 1e Regiment Jagers te Paard on exercise in Germany in the late 1980s. (Eckhard Ude)

their first operational deployments. In 1992 they took part in the US-led Operation Restore Hope in Somalia, continuing in the country for the United Nations' UNOSOM mission the following year. In 1994 they were deployed to Rwanda as part of the UN mission and served in Croatia and Slovenia with UNPROFOR. From March 1999 they participated in KFOR and in 2001 in Operation Joint Guardian in Macedonia. Their final deployment before being retired from service in 2004 was from January to April 2001 as part of the UN peacekeeping intervention in the Second Congo War. Parts of the Belgian CVR(T) fleet were sold to Botswana, Jordan and Ireland.

In all the CVR(T) family has served with the armed forces of 21 other nations besides the United Kingdom and Belgian. The next largest users of the CVR(T) were Iran and Nigeria. Iran purchased some 280 Scorpion before the fall of the Shah in 1979. A large proportion of these were delivered as planned – the remainder being diverted to the RAF Regiment after the Islamic Revolution – and they saw action with limited success during the Iran-Iraq War. Iraq also used several captured Iranian vehicles, and they were maintained by the export of parts to both parties by Alvis during the Iran-Iraq War. The Iraqi Scorpions found their way into the hands of the Jordanians, who also purchased surplus supplies form Belgium and, in 1999, developed their own upgraded Scorpion with the hope of attracting other foreign users of the CVR(T). The Nigerian Army continues to operate between 100 and 150 Scorpion, purchased in the early 1980s and some were upgraded with the Belgian-made OIP-5 fire control system and Cockerill 90mm Mk. III main gun.

The installation of a 90mm main gun on the Scorpion was an attempt to re-equip the vehicle to take on the new generation

(above) A very colourful Nigerian Scorpion on the streets of Lagos.

of armour emerging in the early 1980s. The Cockerill Mk. III gun, manufactured by Belgian firm CMI Defense, fired fin-stabilised, as well as conventional, ammunition from a rifled gun. The new Scorpion, the Scorpion 90 or Scorpion 2, was also fitted with a six-cylinder Perkins diesel engine. One prototype was evaluated and rejected by the British Army, but the version was offered for foreign export in 1980. As well as Nigeria, the Scorpion 90 was purchased by Malaysia (26 vehicles) in 1982, Venezuela (some 50 Scorpion 90, as well as one each of Samson, Samaritan and Sultan) in 1992, and Indonesia (some 90 Scorpion 90 and Stormer APCs) in 1995 and 1996. The Malaysian Scorpion 90s were fitted with German Wegmann 76mm grenade launchers and underwent a Service Life Extension Programme (SLEP) from 2007 and 2011 before being retired in 2018. Plans to replace the 90mm Cockerill gun with a 20mm Oerlikon proved abortive. The Scorpion 90 continues to serve with both the Indonesian and Venezuelan armies.

Another important export customer for the CVR(T) was the Sultanate of Oman. In 1982 they ordered 50 Scorpion as well as three Samson, following this up three years

A Scorpion of the Philippine Army. (Gordon Arthur)

(above) An Irish Scorpion prepares to leave Plunkett Barracks, DFTC (Defence Forces Training Centre) the Curragh Camp, County Kildare. Note the GPMG pintle mount on the front of the turret. (Glen Phelan)

later with an order for 30 more Scorpion. This latter order also included Sultan and Spartan. The Omani Scorpion had several specific modifications. These included the omission of the NBC filtration system in favour of additional 76mm ammunition stowage, a coolant temperature gauge, a new larger rear stowage bin and additional turret stowage bins, the capacity to carry extra jerry cans, a new turret fume extractor, an MG pintle fitted next to the commander's hatch, an air circulation system and numerous other small changes to suit the demands of the Omani military. The gun was also coupled with the L20 Tank Laser Sight to complement the L22 sight fitted to Omani Chieftain MBTs. In 2000 the Omani Scorpions were upgraded with Cummins diesel engine to replace the original Jaguar engines. At present the Royal Omani Army maintains some 37 Scorpion, alongside Spartan, Sultan, Samson and Stormer in service.

The Philippines is another long-time user of the CVR(T). The first 41 Scorpion were delivered in 1977. The Scorpions soldiered on until 2011 when it was decided to upgrade eighteen of the vehicles to the diesel engine after years of indecision. This programme was shelved, however, and fourteen of the Scorpion turrets were transplanted onto M113. Currently, a small number, less than ten, Scorpions remain in service with the Philippine Army but plans are in place to replace them with the Austro-Spanish-designed Sabrah Light Tank. Thailand also maintains a much larger fleet of Scorpion with some 150 still in service, while 76 remain in service with the United Arab Emirates. Smaller numbers of Scorpion remain in service with the armies of Botswana, Brunei, Chile, Honduras, Tanzania, and Togo.

Several countries have now completely retired their CVR(T) fleet. Alongside the United Kingdom and Belgian, the only other NATO member to employ the CVR(T) was Spain. Spain purchased seventeen brand new Scorpions from the UK between 1985 and 1986. They served with Marine Infantry Marine Tercio (Grupo Mecanizado Ampfio-GRUMA) in the role of fire recognition and infantry support. These Scorpions were fitted with diesel engines, and they remained in service until they were retired between 2001 and 2002. They were sold to Chile in 2007 and 2008 to replace Chile's existing ex-British Army Scorpions. Another user of the Scorpion was the Irish Cavalry Corps. In the late 1970s the Irish were still using World War II-vintage Comet tanks, purchased from the UK in 1958. The decision was taken to retire the Comet in 1978 and between March 1980 and December 1985 the Irish purchased fourteen Scorpion. The Irish made several modifications, including a pintle-mounted .50cal M2HB Browning machine gun – later replaced by the smaller General Purpose Machine Gun (GPMG) – and a turret fume

extractor. The Scorpion remained in service with the Irish Cavalry Corps, where they were part of the 1st Armoured Cavalry Squadron, until 2017. The decision was taken not to upgrade the fleet by the then Chief of the Defence Staff, Vice Admiral Mark Mellett, although the idea had been agreed in principle by his predecessor, Lieutenant General Conor O'Boyle. The reconnaissance role was entirely fulfilled by the Swiss-made 8x8 MOWAG Piranha IIIH, which had entered service a decade or so earlier. New Zealand also acquired Scorpion in the early 1980s. By the late 1970s its small fleet of M41 tanks was clearly obsolete and in 1982 they purchased 26 Scorpion from the UK. These served until sold off in 2000.

Beside the UK and Belgian, only one other country has deployed Scimitar. In September 2014 the UK Government agreed to sell 123 surplus Scimitar to Latvia for some £40 million as part of a more general reaffirmation of NATO's commitment to the defence of the Baltic nations in the wake of the Russian annexation of Crimea. The order also included Sultan, Samaritan, Samson and Spartan. 116 CVR(T) are currently deployed with the country's mechanised infantry brigade, while a further seven are used for training. A second agreement has provided for another 82 vehicles to be delivered by 2022.

(above) A rather forlorn looking New Zealand Scorpion. Note the early style solid drive sprocket and the four-colour camouflage scheme based on the American MERDC scheme. (Gordon Arthur)

Latvian Scimitar operate as OPFOR during Exercise Combined Resolve XIII at the Joint Multinational Training Center in Hohenfels, Germany in January 2020. (US Army National Guard photo by Staff Sgt. Gregory Stevens)

(above) 16th/5th The Queen's Royal Lancers replaced 17th/21st Lancers as one of the two Armoured Reconnaissance Regiments of 1 (BR) Corps in October 1974. Here one of their Scimitar is on exercise somewhere in Lower Saxony. Note the flotation screen without the steel cover. (Richard Stickland)

CVR(T) IN ACTION: BAOR AND THE DEFENCE OF EUROPE

In February 1973 A and B Squadrons, the 17th/21st Lancers, based at Northampton Barracks in Wolfenbüttel, Germany, was the first unit in the British Army of the Rhine (BAOR) to receive the new FV101 Scorpion. At first, the squadrons had mixed troops of Scorpion and Ferret, but by the end of the year all three squadrons, included C Squadron which had returned from a demanding tour in Northern Ireland in October, were equipped with the new vehicle. Shortly after 17th/21st Lancers had received their first Scorpions, the other armoured reconnaissance regiment in 1 (British) Corps, 14th/20th Royal Hussars based at Herford, received their new vehicles. In July both regiments took part in their first live-fire exercise at the Hohne ranges (where it was discovered that the blast from Scorpion's 76mm gun tore off the flotation screen). In September and October, A and C Squadrons, 14th/20th Hussars joined with B Squadron, 17th/21st Lancers for Exercise Glory Hawk in the foothills of the Harz Mountains, where the concept of the new fast-moving tracked armoured reconnaissance vehicles was successfully tested before assembled journalists and NATO dignitaries.

These two regiments were the armoured reconnaissance regiments of 1 (British) Corps, the most powerful and lead formation of NATO's Northern Army Group (NORTHAG). This had been established in 1952 for the defence of the north German plain against an invasion by Warsaw Pact (WP) forces. BAOR's operational plan was based on the concept of forward defence: a series of static defensive positions and delaying actions designed to slow down the WP armoured onslaught. In 1973 17th/21st Lancers, for example, were based just ten miles from the Inner German Border (IGB). In the early 1970s, however, NORTHAG in general, and 1 (British) Corps in particular, were ill prepared to fight a conventional war against the WP. The corps within NORTHAG – 1 (Netherlands) Corps, 1 (German) Corps and 1 (Belgium Corps) – had different levels of equipment, training and levels of professionalism, while commander NORTHAG, the peacetime commander of BAOR, had no effective control over the other nations' forces. Moreover, the BAOR suffered from shortages of manpower and equipment, as well as poor morale. Defence spending had been reduced in real terms and the outbreak of the 'Troubles' in Northern Ireland in 1968 had seen soldiers from all arms drawn from BAOR for four-month tours of the province. The lack of an effective operational plan to counter any WP invasion, the successive spending cuts imposed on the Army by the Labour government between 1966 and 1969, and the demands of Operation Banner led the British to, in effect, rely on the NATO's nuclear umbrella to deter any aggression. British and other NATO commanders in NORTHAG were resigned to an early use of tactical and theatre-level nuclear weapons which would almost certainly have quicky escalated to strategic exchange between East and West.The new CVR(T) did not really fit into this idea of static defence.

(above) As well as Germany, British Army CVR(T) served in Norway as part of the Allied Command Europe (ACE) Mobile Force. Here a Scimitar of D Squadron, 13th/18th Royal Hussars (Queen Mary's Own) takes part in Exercise Cold Winter in February 1987. (US Army photo by Cpl. J.D. Gonzales)

Their speed and cross-country ability forced the reconnaissance regiments to rethink their tactics, abandoning the roads and tracks the wheeled Ferret and Saladin had consigned them to in favour of woods and fields. In early 1974 both 17th/21st Lancers and 14th/20th Hussars took delivery of their first Scimitar. This added mobility transformed the potential of the armoured reconnaissance squadrons and the success of the new vehicles led to growing calls for close reconnaissance to be returned to the armoured regiments of BAOR.

In the mid-1970s, largely because of the 1975 Mason Review which saw a further reduction in defence spending and a concentration of conventional forces in Germany, BAOR underwent a major reorganisation. The old three divisions and six brigades order of battle was scrapped in favour of a new, four-armoured division order of battle alongside the brigade-sized 5th Field Force. The first division to be restructured was 2nd Armoured Division in the autumn of 1976, with 1st and 4th Armoured Divisions similarly restructured during the following year. In January 1978 3rd Division was moved to Germany from the UK as 3rd Armoured Division. Initially each division was given two armoured regiments, three mechanised infantry battalions and an armoured reconnaissance regiment organised into task forces, flexible units that could be assigned tank squadrons and mechanised infantry battalions as the tactical need dictated. Alongside the CVR(T) of the armoured reconnaissance

(below) This well-used Scorpion is typical of the appearance of the CVR(T) of the Armoured Reconnaissance Regiments and reconnaissance troops of 1 (BR) Corps in the late 1980s. Note the additional stowage boxes added to address the chronic shortage of storage space in the original design. (Eckhard Ude)

(above) The white cross on this Scorpion shows that it is an umpires' vehicle in one of the many field training exercises in which Bagnall's new operational plan for 1 (BR) Corps was refined during the late 1980s. (Eckhard Ude)

regiments, Scorpion and Scimitar served in the reconnaissance troops of the armoured regiments (although the FV102 Striker ATGM was reassigned to separate Royal Horse Artillery batteries where they remained until 1984). 5th Field Force, the former 24th Infantry Brigade, was moved from Catterick to Osnabrück in 1977 and initially assigned 2nd Royal Tank Regiment as its armoured reconnaissance regiment. Thus, in the late 1970s BAOR had eight armoured regiments, three fewer than it had under the old organisation, but five armoured reconnaissance regiments (one for each division and another in 5th Field Force) and close reconnaissance troops in each armoured regiment.

Despite this reorganisation, in the late 1970s BAOR's ability to play its role as 1 (British) Corps in NORTHAG was seriously in doubt. The economic situation at home, severe shortages of manpower and equipment, and the continued demands of the Troubles, all contributed to low morale and preparedness for war. Indeed, the idea of Forward Defence that governed NATO's strategy and the basic British idea of fighting retreats conducted by independent Battle Groups, combined with the superiority in men and equipment enjoyed by the WP troops facing 1 (British) Corps across the IGB, meant that the early use of nuclear weapons was as likely in the late 1970s as it had been a decade earlier. In 1981 the Task Forces were disbanded and the divisions of BAOR were once again reformed into brigades, while 5th Field Force was disbanded and the soldiers returned to the United Kingdom. This was part of the 1981 Defence Review, *The Way Forward*, which saw a further reduction in defence spending as the recession bit. The Army escaped the bulk of the reductions as the Conservative government favoured the defence of Europe over Britain's maritime commitments, but BAOR would have to make do with less. However, under the energetic and reforming leadership of General Sir Nigel Bagnall, appointed to command 1 (British) Corps in November 1980, the fighting abilities of BAOR and NORTHAG were transformed over the next decade.

Bagnall's reforms were based on the premise that NORTHAG must operate in wartime as a whole, and not as a group of independent national army corps, in order to successfully resist any WP aggression, eventually defeating the enemy in a conventional battle and avoiding the apocalyptic resort to nuclear weapons. In 1983 Bagnall began a major reorganisation of 1 (British) Corps. 1st and 4th Armoured Divisions were restructured with three armoured brigades each, while 3rd Armoured Division was assigned an additional infantry brigade from the UK. 2nd Armoured Division was renamed 2nd Infantry Division and relocated its headquarters to York in January 1983. Consisting largely of Territorial Amy (TA) Units, it would be 1 (British) Corps' reserve division, transported to Germany in the event of war. Each of the three armoured divisions retained an armoured reconnaissance regiment, while the infantry brigades of the 2nd Infantry Divisions had the close reconnaissance role fulfilled by the TA Yeomanry regiments equipped with the wheeled FV721 Fox armoured car.

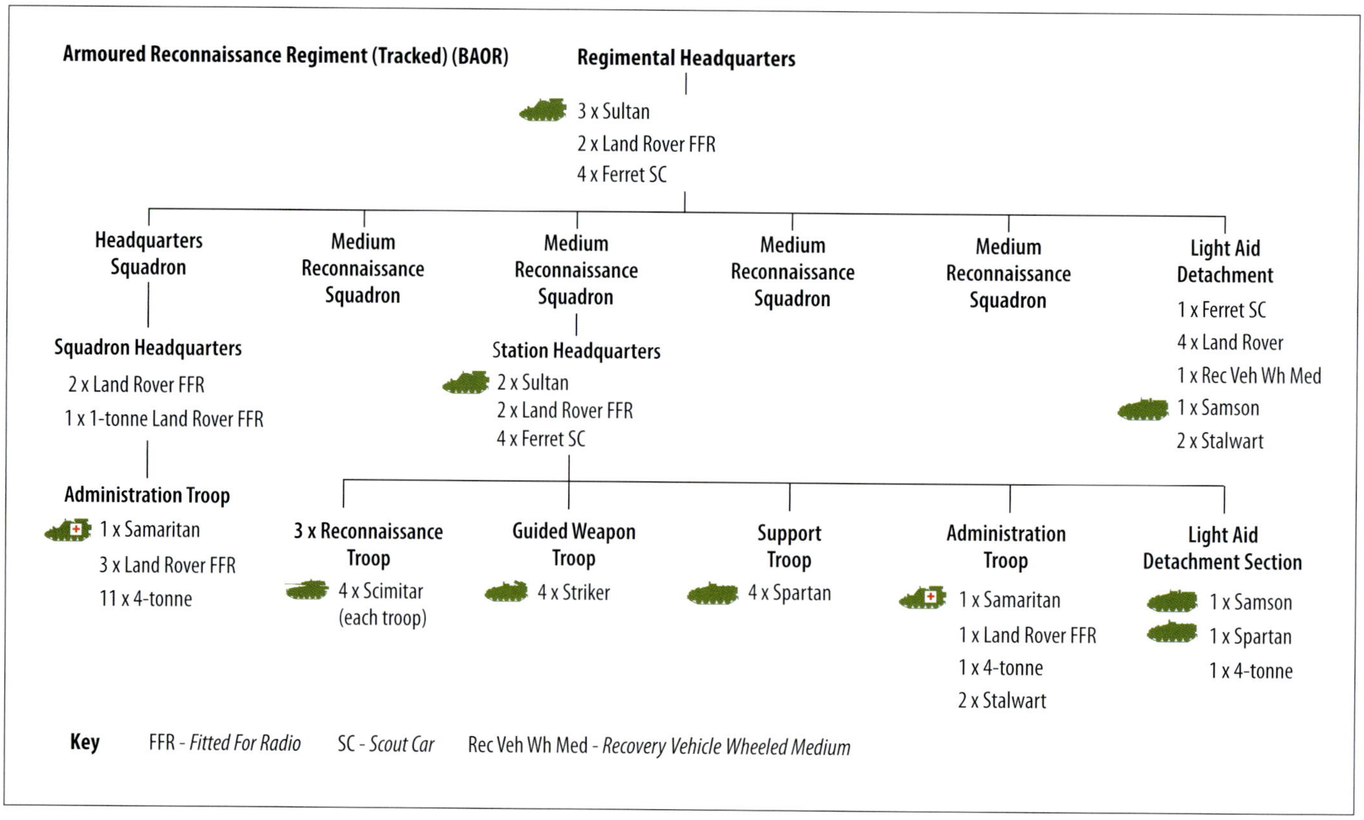

(above) The organisation of the Germany-based Armoured Reconnaissance Regiments of 1 (BR) Corps from 1983. The UK-based Armoured Reconnaissance regiments had mixed troops of Scimitar and Scorpion in their Sabre Squadrons.

From the mid 1980s NATO's ability to withstand and defeat a WP attack by conventional forces alone was transformed. In NORTHAG Bagnall developed his own version of the American AirLand Battle doctrine, using air power and long-range artillery to destroy the WP's second echelon units, while using fast-moving manoeuvre warfare to isolate and defeat the WP first echelon. Forward Defence gave way to a more flexible defence, ceding territory in order to extend WP supply lines. New weapon systems played an important role in this new operational plan. From 1983 Challenger began to replace the Chieftain as the main battle tank in BAOR, while three years later the first mechanised infantry battalions received the new FV510 Warrior Infantry Fighting Vehicle. The CVR(T) family as a whole was already perfectly suited to the more mobile defence advocated by Bagnall. The new organisation was tested for the first time in Exercise Lionheart in 1984, the largest peacetime deployment of British Army, and refined through a series of field training exercises at the Corps level over the next few years, working with NATO partners both in NORTHAG and with the US V Corps, that led to greater interoperability across all the armies involved in the defence of West Germany.

In November 1989 the Berlin Wall was torn down, marking the symbolic end of the Cold War. In 1991, when the Soviet Union collapsed, there were still some 300,000 soldiers and over 4,000 troops stationed in East Germany, but over the next three years they returned to Russia. Ultimately, the success of Bagnall's reforms was seen during the First Gulf, and the 1992 Defence Review, *Options for Change*, greatly reduced the armoured strength of the British Army.

On 1 October 1992 1 (British) Corps was officially disbanded, forming instead the core of Allied Command Europe Rapid Reaction Corps. When BAOR itself was disbanded on 31 March 1994, only 4th Armoured Division, renamed 1st (UK) Armored Division, remained in Germany. It consisted of three armoured brigades, with the Light Dragoons initially providing the Formation Reconnaissance Regiment (FRR). In August 2000 they were replaced by 9th/12th Royal Lancers, who in turn were replaced in September 2003 by 1st The Queen's Dragoon Guards when they deployed to Iraq as part of Operation Telic. In 2004 another defence review, *Delivering Security in a Changing World*, saw a further reduction of the British Army's armoured strength. This allowed for one additional CVR(T)-equipped FRR in the UK (giving three in total, including the Household Cavalry Regiment), and two FRR, one for each of the two remaining armoured brigades of 1st (UK) Armoured Division, remaining in Germany. In 2015 the last Scimitar-equipped regiment in Germany, 9th/12th Royal Lancers, returned to the Catterick to be amalgamated with the Queen's Royal Lancers to form the Royal Lancers (Queen Elizabeth's Own). The regiment still operates Scimitar and in October 2021 returned to Germany, supplying the Divisional Reconnaissance Battle Group in the multi-national NATO exercise Somme Lancer.

CVR(T) IN ACTION: THE FALKLANDS WAR

On 2 April 1982 Argentina invaded and quickly conquered the Falkland Islands, a small British territory in the South Atlantic. Three days later the British government decided to send a combined arms taskforce to the South Atlantic to retake the islands by force should the international diplomatic efforts to settle the conflict peaceably fail. Among the units attached to 3 Commando Brigade were 3 and 4 Troop, B Squadron, The Blues and Royals. They set sail from Plymouth aboard the ocean liner SS *Canberra* a week later with four Scimitar, four Scorpion and a REME section Sultan. The deployment came as a not unwelcome surprise to the 25 men and two officers who barely had time to collect their winter kit and pay their mess bills before setting sail. On reaching Ascension Island and after having practised gunnery, they carried onto the South Atlantic aboard HMS *Fearless*, before making the landing in support of 3rd Battalion, The Parachute Regiment at San Carlos on 21 May.

On East Falkland the CVR(T) was in its element. The extraordinarily low ground pressure of its tracks confounded those who said armoured vehicles would be rendered useless in the peaty bogs of the Falklands Islands and the men of 4 Troop were soon employed in the reconnaissance role as 3 Para advanced to Teal Inlet. Instead of the allotted three days, the Troop reached the inlet within a day, pushing onto to Estancia Hill where they gained their first sight of the capital, Port Stanley. At nearby Mount Kent, the Scorpions of 4 Troop engaged dug-in Argentine infantry with indirect fire from their 76mm. On 8 June 4 Troop witnessed the disastrous sinking of RFA *Sir Galahad* and *Sir Tristram* in Bluff Cove. One of the troop's Scimitars was credited with shooting down an Argentine A-4 Skyhawk with its 30mm Rarden cannon. Meanwhile, on 13 June, 3 Troop supported 2 Para's assault on Wireless Ridge, using their Scimitar's 30mm cannon to destroy enemy bunkers. On the same night 4 Troop was with the 2nd Battalion, The Scots Guards on Mount Tumbledown. Moving forward to provide fire support, The Blues and Royal suffered their only vehicle loss when Lieutenant Coreth's Scorpion hit a mine. Luckily, the crew escaped with nothing more than shock, but the vehicle was put out of action. The Argentinians were soon in full retreat towards Stanley and the invaders surrendered the following day. While 3 Troop moved into Stanley, the unfortunate 4 Troop remained in the field awaiting the Argentine counterattack that never materialised.

The CVR(T) had proved itself a valuable asset to the Taskforce both in the reconnaissance role and in direct support of infantry operations. The effectiveness of light armour in supporting infantry was not lost on those present and the refusal of Lieutenant-Colonel 'H' Jones's request for armoured support at Goose Green may have contributed to 2 Para's heavy casualties there on 27-28 May. If the whole of B Squadron had deployed to the South Atlantic victory on the Falkland Islands may have been both swifter and achieved with less loss of life on both sides.

(below) In 1999 the US Army's 'Armor' journal ran an article considering the contribution of the CVR(T) to British victory in the Falklands. They concluded that 'the overwhelming firepower and shock effect' of the Scorpion and Scimitar was an important lesson for future combined arms operations. (US Army)

CVR(T) IN ACTION: OPERATION GRANBY

As the Cold War ended and the United Kingdom began to think about the role of its armoured force in the future, the CVR(T) family faced its sternest test of combat to date. On 2 August 1990 Iraqi forces invaded Kuwait. Within 48 hours the Emir had fled, the Kuwaiti armed forces had either surrendered or escaped to Saudi Arabia, and a coalition of nations, led by the United States, was organising to demand the Iraqis withdraw from what Saddam Hussein would soon declare 'the nineteenth province of Iraq'. The invasion had been planned long in advance and the warning signs largely ignored by the Kuwaitis and their allies. At the time Iraq had the fourth largest army in the world and their soldiers had recent combat experience in the long and bloody Iran-Iraq War, which had ended just two years previously. Nevertheless, they would prove ineffective against the vast international coalition that was soon assembled against them.

On 26 October the men and vehicles of the British 7 Armoured Brigade Group arrived in Jubayl in Saudi Arabia. As well as the eight Scorpions in each reconnaissance troop of the two tank regiments – The Royal Scots Dragoon Guards and The Queen's Royal Irish Hussars – medium reconnaissance was provided by A Squadron, 1st The Queen's Dragoon Guards (QDG) with its sixteen Scimitar. Initially the brigade was placed under the command of the US 1st Marine Division. Early in January 1991, 7 Armoured Brigade was joined by 4 Armoured Brigade. This consisted of one tank regiment (14th/20th King's Hussars), two mechanised infantry battalions (1st Battalion, The Royal Scots and 3rd Battalion, The Royal Regiment of Fusiliers) and the Regimental HQ and three Sabre squadrons of the 16th/5th, The Queen's Royal Lancers (QRL), the armoured reconnaissance regiment of 1st (UK) Armoured Division stationed in Herford, Germany. It brought 24 Scimitar, 24 Scorpion and sixteen Strikers to the Gulf. The mechanised infantry battalions of 4 Armoured Brigade also had eight Scimitar each in their reconnaissance platoons. Other CVR(T) served in Royal Artillery and Royal Engineer units. As well as those of the British Army, Scorpion and Spartan of 1 Squadron, RAF Regiment were deployed from Germany to provide security for Al Qaysumah and Muharraq airbases. They subsequently joined 7 Armoured Brigade for the final push into Kuwait In all 503 CVR(T) were deployed to the Gulf as part of Operation Granby, comprising 238 Spartan (many in the air defence role carrying teams of Javelin SAM operators), 101 Scimitar, 33 Scorpion, 24 Sultan, 22 Striker, 23 MCT Spartan, 20 Samaritan and four Stormer VLMSS.

The armoured reconnaissance regiments of BAOR, as we have seen, were designed for reconnaissance by stealth, moving fast and close to the enemy. Crucially, their training had naturally focused on reconnaissance in defence, not for the large armoured formation offensive that would be necessary to liberate Kuwait. As a result, the QRL, with the squadron

A Scorpion of the Reconnaissance Troop of The Royal Scots Dragoon Guards in southern Iraq on 28 February 1991 during Operation Desert Sabre. Note the high-visibility air recognition panel and black inverted V theatre marking designed to guard against 'blue-on-blue' attacks. (US Army photo by PHC Holmes)

A Samaritan armoured ambulance and FV432 of the HQ Squadron, The Royal Scots Dragoon Guards in southern Iraq. (US Army photo by PHC Holmes)

from QDG attached, was placed under the command of the 1st (UK) Armoured Division's Commander of Artillery. Along with the 210mm M110A2 self-propelled howitzers and Multiple Rocket Launch Systems of the Royal Artillery and Forward Air Controllers, it was to form a General Support/Recce Strike Group whose role was to scout for and engage enemy formations in depth, preventing them from moving forward to reinforce Iraqi units facing the tank and mechanised infantry units of 4 and 7 Armoured Brigade.

The Coalition offensive, Operation Desert Sabre, began on 25 February 1991 and the Recce Strike Group crossed the start line at 15:00, well after the tanks had begun their advance. By midnight the following day, QRL had advanced some 80 kilometres into Iraq. The next morning, they engaged enemy positions at Objective Lead (all the identified Iraqi concentrations were named after metals). Soon the Scimitars were engaging Iraqi T-55s with their 30mm cannon with limited success, but the Swingfire missiles of the Strikers accounted for several enemy AFVs. Crucially, however, the CVR(T) were able to successfully call in artillery and airstrikes to break the concentrations of Iraqi armour that threatened the Coalition manoeuvre brigades.

Following their success at Objective Lead, the QDG were given the task of leading 7 Armoured Brigade's advance into Kuwait, while QRL, supported by D Squadron, 14th/20th Hussars, attacked an Iraqi position identified as Objective Tungsten. Royal Engineer Spartans identified a suitable crossing point, making a sand rampart over the three-metre-tall pipeline that ran across that particular part of the desert. The ensuing battle lasted four hours with the CVR(T) of the Reconnaissance Group at the fore.

No CVR(T) were lost to enemy action during Operation Desert Sabre, although a Scimitar of C Squadron, QRL, was temporarily abandoned after its 30mm ammunition was set on fire by 12.7mm machine gun rounds fired by an Iraqi T-55. On 27 February two Scorpion of The Queen's Royal Irish Hussars were lost when they were engaged in error by M1A1 Abrams of the US 2nd Cavalry Regiment. Miraculously only two crewmen were slightly wounded.

The CVR(T) had proved itself a valuable component of the Coalition force despite its age and the shortcomings of some of its equipment. The lack of proper integrated thermal imaging equipment hampered the Scorpion's and Scimitar's ability to perform at night and in poor weather. Crew were frequently forced to exit their vehicles and use the OTIS sight manually or employ hand-held Spyglass thermal imagers. Shortly after arriving in Saudi Arabia the CVR(T) were equipped with Trimpack or Magellan GPS systems, which proved invaluable in the featureless desert of southern Iraq. The Clansmen radio systems were also upgraded with the installation of BID300. Despite the challenge posed by the sands of Saudi Arabia or the hard gravel of southern Iraq, the CVR(T) surprised some by its mechanical reliability. Good logistics and a constant supply of spare parts kept the availability rate of the CVR(T) fleet to some 80 per cent.

CVR(T) IN ACTION: KEEPING THE PEACE

There is an almost certainly apocryphal story that, during the planning stage, it was stipulated that the width of the CVR(T) should not exceed 84 inches as this was the width of the paths between trees in the rubber plantations of Malaysia, wide enough for a fully laden elephant to pass unhindered. Whatever truth lies in this tale, it does, nevertheless, highlight the fact that during the 1960s the British Army still had at least one eye on the low-intensity, counter insurgency wars that had characterised its experience in the years after World War II. Given its light weight, mobility and the firepower it offers without the political impact of a main battle tank, Scorpion and Scimitar have played an important role in the various peacekeeping and unconventional conflicts the British Army has found itself embroiled in since the 1970s.

In July 1974 the Regimental Headquarters and A Squadron, 16th/5th The Queen's Royal Lancers were ordered to go with their Scorpion to Cyprus to defend British interests after the Turkish invasion of the north of the island. In fact, the Scorpions remained at the British Sovereign Base Area Dhekilia and the job of evacuating and protecting British civilians was left to the Ferrets and Saladin armoured cars that were already with the British contingent stationed there. A longer, and perhaps more meaningful, employment began in 1976 when a troop of Scorpion from B Squadron, The Life Guards were deployed to British Honduras in central America to guard against invasion by neighbouring Honduras. The mission to British Honduras – or Belize as it became known after independence in September 1981 – was threefold: to counter any possible Honduran invasion, to attempt to police the border against the heavily armed drug gangs that operated throughout central America, and to learn jungle warfare skills in the 550 square miles granted to the British Army as a training area by the grateful Belizean government. The Armoured Reconnaissance Regiments took it in turns to provide a troop to man the Belize Scorpions for a six-month tour. It was a demanding tour in some ways. The vehicles were not well maintained and there was a shortage of spare parts. When the 17th/21st Lancers arrived in September 1979 they found only three of the six Scorpion operational and it took several weeks, with the crews working round the clock, to get all back in service. Trees felled by the drug gangs made jungle patrols difficult, but overall, a posting to Belize was a welcome relief from the rigours of Northern Ireland or the monotony of Germany.

The most challenging peacekeeping missions that the British Army was involved in were the various conflicts that marked the collapse of the former Yugoslavia. Between 1992, when British troops were first sent to Bosnia for Operation Grapple under a United Nations mandate, and 2000, when the final armoured contingents were sent to Kosovo, the CVR(T) played an important role in the UN and later NATO efforts to keep and then impose by force peace in the former Yugoslavia. In November 1992 Scimitar from 1st Battalion, The Cheshire Regiment, and B Squadron, the 9th/12th Royal Lancers, deployed to Bosnia as part of the United Nations Protection

One of the Belize Scorpions operated by 17th/21st Lancers during their tour in 1979-80. Note the 'Cassino II' marking. This tradition of naming CVR(T) after one of a regiment's battle honours was carried one by regiments deployed to the Balkans. (Andy Bulpett)

A Scimitar of the HCR plays host to two Dutch officers during a parade at Banja Luka in 1996. (MoD Crown Copyright)

Force (UNPROFOR). The task of the white-painted CVR(T) of BRITBAT was to protect humanitarian routes and aid convoys from Bosnian Serb aggression. In May 1993 B Squadron, The Light Dragoons, and 1st Battalion, The Prince of Wales's Own Regiment of Yorkshire deployed to Bosnia. As conditions and Serb aggression increased, so did the British Army's commitment and by the following year two squadrons and the RHQ of The Light Dragoons was in country.

In 1995, as peace negotiations between the warring factions failed, NATO decided to intervene military to stop a humanitarian catastrophe in Bosnia. From December, as part of NATO's Implementation Force (IFOR), a brigade-strength formation was deployed as the core of Multi-National Division (South-West), based at Banja Luka. As part of Operation Resolute, as the British termed it, 4 Mechanised Brigade, 1 Mechanised Brigade and 20 Armoured Brigade, with their organic Armoured Reconnaissance Regiments, were deployed to Bosnia. In December 1996 NATO's mission changed to the Stabilisation Force (SFOR) and as part of Operation Lodestar, 7 Armoured Brigade deployed there in April 1997, with 9th/12th Royal Lancers returning to Bosnia in the armoured reconnaissance role. The Scimitar proved itself useful in Bosnia, where it was a less threatening presence than the larger and more heavily armoured Warrior IFV. Although it had greater mobility than Warrior, it still struggled in the snow and ice of the Bosnian winter and some units preferred the humble Land Rover fitted with snow chains over the CVR(T) for reconnaissance patrols.

No sooner had relative stability returned to Bosnia, then the focus of ethnic tension moved to Kosovo. In the summer of 1998 activities by the Kosovo Liberation Army (KLA) led to reprisals by the Yugoslavian and Serbian military, largely aimed against Kosovo's Albanian Muslim population. In October NATO launched limited airstrikes against Yugoslav targets, but the fighting in Kosovo, and the atrocities, intensified. The failure of peace talks led to a much more sustained and intense NATO air campaign, which lasted from March until June 1999. On 10 June NATO suspended its air campaign when Yugoslavia agreed to withdraw from Kosovo and two days later NATO's Kosovo Force (KFOR) arrived to separate the warring parties and enforce peace. Operation Agricola, the British Army's deployment as part of KFOR, consisted of 4 Armoured Brigade, with the Household Cavalry Regiment (HCR), already in Bosnia as part of SFOR, providing armoured reconnaissance. A Scimitar of the HCR was the first British vehicle to enter Pristina, the Kosovan capital, on 12 June and, with the withdrawal of Serb forces, the British were given responsibility for a 400km^2 area of Kosovo from Pristina to the Serbian border. The mission was a difficult one for as well as guarding against Serb insurgency, the British Army was also required to protect the minority Serb population of Kosovo against violence from the ethnic Albanians. The deployments in the Balkans once again demonstrated the effectiveness of the Scimitar and the versatility of the whole CVR(T) family.

CVR(T) IN ACTION: IRAQ AND AFGHANISTAN

On 20 March 2003 some 175,000 Coalition military personnel, including over 32,000 grounds troops from the United Kingdom, invaded Iraq. Operation Telic, as the UK's involvement in Iraq was known, lasted until July 2009 and cost the lives of 179 UK service personnel and over £9 billion of taxpayers' money. The initial offensive to defeat Saddam Hussein lasted just 41 days and on 1 May President George W. Bush announced "mission completed". Yet before long the invasion had deteriorated into a long and bloody insurgency which would not end even with the final withdrawal of Coalition troops in 2011.

For the invasion itself 1st (UK) Armoured Division was deployed to the Gulf, comprising 7 Armoured Brigade and 16 Air Assault Brigade, while 3 Commando Brigade also came under divisional command. The deployment time was considerably quicker than in 1990 – ten weeks compared to 22 weeks – and saw over a thousand AFVs arrive in Saudi Arabia, including 155 CVR(T)s and six Stormer minelaying vehicles. Scimitar and other CVR(T)s served with the Formation Reconnaissance Regiment, 1st The Queen's Dragoon Guards (QDG), while D Squadron, The Household Cavalry Regiment (HCR) was attached to 16 Air Assault Brigade.

Initially, D Squadron, HCR covered the Royal Engineers' breaching of the massive sand berm on the Iraqi Border and then reconnoitred the route to the Rumayllah oilfields for the US Marine Corps (UMSC) 5th Marine Regiment, the vanguard of the US 1st Marine Division. From there the separate troops of D Squadron carried out traditional close reconnaissance tasks, supporting the advance of both 16 Air Assault Brigade and the USMC in southern Iraq. This involved negotiating the treacherous irrigation channels and the larger canals and waterways around the main Baghdad to Basra highway. The HCR's experiences are captured in graphic detail in the account *Bullet Magnet* written by Lance Corporal of Horse Mick Flynn. Flynn's Scimitar successfully engaged and destroyed Iraqi BMP-1s and T-55s of the Iraqi 4th Armoured Division, but he also recounts the 'blue-on-blue' incident when HCR Scimitars were mistakenly engaged by an American A-10 and one crew member killed and three seriously injured, as well as the tragic death of Lieutenant Alex Tweedie whose Scimitar slipped off the road and into one of the drainage canals and overturned.

QDG supported 3 Commando Brigade during the battle for Basra itself. On 30 March British forces launched Operation James to take Abu al-Khasib, an important suburb of the city. Scimitars of C Squadron, QDG supported 40 Royal Marine Commando's assault, a cooperation later recognised by the award of the Commando Dagger to C Squadron. Throughout the initial combat phase of Operation Telic, the CVR(T) again proved itself an effective weapon of war. It proved generally reliable with between 74 and 100 per cent of CVR(T) variants available from 21 March to 30 April, although Warrior, Challenger 2, AS90 and the venerable FV430 all delivered slightly greater levels of combat readiness, and a number of vehicles were cannibalised to keep the fleet operational.

In July 2003 19 Mechanised Brigade moved to Iraq as part of Operation Telic II with close reconnaissance provided by elements of The Light Dragoons and The Queen's Royal Lancers. They were in turn replaced by 20 Armoured Brigade in November that year and 9th/12th Royal Lancers in the Formation Reconnaissance role. In all, there were twelve roulements of British troops deployed as part of Operation Telic up to April 2009 and the Scimitar, variously upgraded and modified to meet the challenges of service in Iraq, played an important role throughout.

As the British Army's mission in Iraq lessened in intensity, that in Afghanistan began to grow. British troops had been in that troubled country since 2001 but in 2006 it was announced that Operation Herrick, as the British involvement in Afghanistan was called, was to be expanded as part of ISAF's (International Security Assistance Force) mission in Helmand Province. In April 2006

A Scimitar of D Squadron, The Household Cavalry Regiment, supports an AAVP of 5th Marine Regiment, USMC, at the beginning of the invasion of Iraq in March 2003. (USMC photo by Sgt. Kevin R. Reed)

D Squadron, HCR deployed to Helmand as part of Operation Herrick IV with 16 Air Assault Brigade. In August Scimitars and other CVR(T) of D Squadron were tasked with relieving British soldiers under siege in the Hellmand town of Musa Qal'ah. On the approach to the town, one of the HCR Spartan was lost to a mine, but in the town itself the Scimitars were ambushed by well-equipped and determined Taliban fighters in pre-prepared positions. One Spartan was knocked out by RPG fire, but the Scimitars survived numerous RPG and heavy machine gun hits to eventually rout the Taliban. LCpl of Horse Flynn, who was awarded the Military Cross for his bravery at Musa Qal'ah, once again provides a graphic and moving account of the action in his autobiography. The effectiveness of the 30mm Rarden cannon and of the up-armouring of the Scimitar as a result of lessons learnt in Iraq was again proved in battle. Thereafter up to four close reconnaissance squadrons at a time from a variety of different regiments were deployed to Hellmand until the final deployment of B Squadron, The Light Dragoons as the Force Reconnaissance Squadron for Operation Herrick XVI between May and October 2012.

(above) A Squadron, the 9th/12th Royal Lancers deployed to Iraq in November 2003 as part of Operation Telic III. Their Scimitar had the newly fitted Plasan additional armour. (Carl Schulze)

The entire operational CVR(T) family with numerous upgrades resulting from the various Urgent Operational Requirements were deployed to Hellmand. These were in part driven by the mechanical frailties that the harsh environment of Hellmand exposed, as well as the need to provide enhanced protection against mines and IEDs. Tactics and the Formation Reconnaissance role also evolved during Operation Herrick as new vehicles, such as the Jackal Tactical Support Vehicle (TSV), were introduced into Task Force Hellmand. For Herrick XVI, for example, B Squadron, The Light Dragoons operated as three sabre troops with Scimitar 2, a support troop with Spartan 2, and a Force Support Group troop equipped with TSV.

(below) A Squadron, the 9th/12th Royal Lancers also deployed to Afghanistan between May and October 2011 with Operation Herrick XIV. Here you can see the bar armour and other additions of the Environmental Mitigation Urgent Operational Requirement (EM UOR) package fitted to the Scimitar 235. (Carl Schulze)

A Scimitar of 1st The Queen's Dragoon Guards during Exercise Bavarian Charger held in the summer of 2013 at the Grafenwoehr Training Area. (MoD Crown Copyright photograph by Cpl Wes Calder RLC)

CVR(T) TODAY

Fifty years is a very long time for any piece of military hardware to remain in service. Few weapons can boast such a heritage as the CVR(T) family and probably only the Ferret armoured car and the FV430 series can claim a longer history in the British Army. To use an armoured fighting vehicle analogy, it is akin to the M4 Sherman or T-34 remaining in frontline service from 1941 until the end of the Cold War.

Today the CVR(T) remains in service with the British Army as the main weapons system of the two armoured cavalry regiments of the Royal Armoured Corps (RAC): The Royal Dragoon Guards and The Royal Lancers (Queen Elizabeth's Own). Both operate Scimitar, alongside Spartan and the Panther Protected Patrol Vehicle. The other reconnaissance regiments of the British Army – The Light Dragoons, 1st The Queen's Dragoon Guards, and The Royal Scots Dragoon Guards – are configured as light cavalry regiments, equipped with the Jackal 2 and Coyote Tactical Support Vehicles. The final RAC regiment in the reconnaissance role, the Household Cavalry Regiment, has been repurposed as an armoured reconnaissance regiment equipped with the CVR(T)'s successor, the Ajax. The British Army currently still has some 200 CVR(T) in service.

Finding a replacement for the CVR(T) has been a long and difficult process. Since the 1980s there has been a string of failed and abandoned projects to provide a replacement armoured reconnaissance capability for the British Army. Since the end of the Cold War these have included the Tactical Reconnaissance Combat Equipment Requirement (TRACER) commenced in May 1992 and cancelled in October 2001 at a cost of £131 million; the Multi-Role Armoured Vehicle (MRAV), commissioned in March 1998 and cancelled five years later at a cost of £57 million; and the Future Rapid Effect System (FRES) Scout vehicle, which eventually evolved into AJAX after some twenty years of development.

In 2015 the UK Government announced plans for a £4.5 billion programme to produce a total of 589 tracked armoured vehicles to replace all variants of the CVR(T) and provide reconnaissance, command and control, equipment repair, and combat engineering capability across a single platform: AJAX. AJAX would form the core of the British Army's new Strike Brigades with each Strike Brigade having two AJAX-equipped regiments, each with some 50-60 vehicles. The Army would have an Initial Operating Capability by 2021 and full operational readiness by 2025. AJAX would be one of the best-protected and heaviest armoured reconnaissance vehicles in the world, with the then Chief of the Defence Staff describing it as 'completely different capability' to the existing CVR(T). The first hundred AJAX were to be assembled in Spain, before assembly was moved to a new plant in Merthyr Tydfil. In 2018 the total whole-life cost for Ajax was given as £6.2 billion. The first Strike Brigade was designed to be 1 Armoured Infantry Brigade with both HCR and The Royal Dragoon Guards converting to AJAX from Scimitar. A second Strike Brigade would see The Royal Lancers give up their CVR(T), while The King's Royal Hussars would convert from Challenger 2 to AJAX.

The AJAX programme continued to experience problems with HCR reporting serious problems with the noise and vibration experienced by the crews which lead to all testing being suspended in the summer of 2021. In September that year the government announced that 'is not possible to determine a realistic timescale

Scimitar of the Household Cavalry Regiment pause in the Omani desert during Exercise Saif Sareea in November 2018. (MoD Crown Copyright)

for the introduction of AJAX vehicles into operational service.' Nevertheless, despite these problems, the political pressure not to abandon AJAX remains considerable. In November 2021 the Ministry of Defence published its *Future Soldier* document, outlining the proposed structure of the British Army into the next decade. This undertook to deliver a warfighting division by 2030 with AJAX very much part of an integrated suite of armoured fighting vehicles including the upgraded Challenger 3 MBT and the Boxer Mechanised Infantry Vehicle. In this new structure in 1st (UK) Division, The Royal Scots Dragoon Guards will have the light cavalry role in 7th Light Mechanised Brigade Combat Team, while the Light Dragoons will do the same for 4th Light Brigade Combat Team. Two more reserve yeomanry regiments would also be in the light cavalry role. In 3rd (UK) Division, the principal combat formation of the Field Army, The King's Royal Hussars, equipped with AJAX, will operate as the armoured cavalry regiment in 12th Armoured Brigade Combat Team, while The Royal Dragoon Guards will perform the same role in 20th Armoured Brigade Combat Team. The HCR and The Royal Lancers will operate AJAX as the armoured cavalry regiments of the newly formed 1st Deep Recce Strike Brigade Combat Team, with 1st The Queen's Dragoon Guards in the light cavalry role.

The Future Soldier programme spells the end of the CVR(T) in the British Army and the last Scimitar and Spartan will be withdrawn from service by 2023 as part of these plans. Spanning six decades of service, the success of the CVR(T) family is partly testimony to the engineering excellence of the British defence industry, but principally to the adaptability, resilience and skill of the British soldiers who have served in it during those years.

Ajax will replace Scimitar as the principal weapons system in the four armoured cavalry regiments of the British Army from 2023. (MoD Crown Copyright)

Further Reading

Simon Dunstan's Osprey title on the Scorpion and Scimitar, *Scorpion Reconnaissance Vehicle* (Osprey New Vanguard 13), is probably still the most accessible introduction to the history of the CVR(T), complemented by his *Scorpion CVR(T) Owners' Workshop Manual* (Haynes 2021). A good collection of photographs of early CVR(T) can be found in the same author's *Scorpion: the CVR(T) Range* (Tanks Illustrated 22: Arms and Armour Press, 1986). George Forty's *The Scorpion Family* (Modern Combat Vehicles 5: Ian Allan Ltd, 1983) remains a good account of the early development of the family. More recently *Daniel Nowak's CVR(T) Scorpion – Scimitar – Sabre* (Tankograd British Special 9033) and *CVR(T) Other Variants* (Tankograd British Special 9034) are superb, bringing the CVR(T) story up to date. For a rare insight into the combat service of the CVR(T) written by a veteran of the Falklands War and the wars in Iraq and Afghanistan see Mick Flynn, *Bullet Magnet* (Weidenfeld & Nicolson, 2010). For extensive walkarounds of the CVR(T) family, Michael Shackleton's *CVR(T) Family* (Trackpad Publishing, 2018). Part 1 covers the Scorpion, Scimitar and Striker, while Part 2 covers Spartan, Sultan, Samaritan and Samson and both are peerless in their level of detail and utility to the modeller.

There are a number of excellent photo albums that will provide further information and inspiration to modellers contemplating a CVR(T) project:

Bob Morrison, *Scorpion and the CVR(T) Family* (Concord Publications, 1994)

Daniel Nowak, *Recce: The Eyes and Ears of 1st (UK) Armoured Division* (Tankograd British Special 9011)

John Prigent, *Scorpion, Scimitar and Sabre* (Museum Ordnance Special 23, 1998)

Carl Schulze, *British Armour Evolution* (Tankograd British Special 9005)

Carl Schulze, *Task Force Hellmand: Vehicles of the British ISAF Forces in Afghanistan 2011* (Tankograd British Special 9017)

There are also some excellent images of various CVR(T) scattered throughout the various books in Tankograd's British Special Series. The *Journal of Armored Assault & Heliborne Warfare Volume 11* (Concord Publications, 2005) contains a wonderful collection of images of CVR(T) of the 9th/12th Royal Lancers on exercise in Germany immediately prior to their deployment to Iraq, while Volume 17 (Concord Publications, 2006) of the same has extensive coverage of Belgian Scimitars and other CVR(T).

Thanks to Mark Smith, Gordon Arthur, JW de Boer, Christian Bray, Peter Brown, Andy Bulpett, Paul Crocker, Claudio Fernandez, Chris Jerrett, Alan Ng, Glen Phelan, MP Robinson, Carl Schulze, Michael Shackleton, Kevin Shannon, Richard Stickland, Eckhard Ude and Patrick Winnepenninckx for their help and encouragement in putting this volume together.

A Belgian FV101 Scorpion of 1st Jagers te Paard during Field Training Exercise Crossed Swords in 1986. Note the flotation screen still in place, as well as the early solid drive sprocket and rear idler wheel. (Belgian Armed Forces Archives via Christian Bray)